Rethink the Business of Creativity

Copyright © 2020 by
Rethink Communications
rethinkcanada.com

20 21 22 23 24   5 4 3 2 1

All rights reserved. No part of this
book may be reproduced, stored in
a retrieval system, or transmitted,
in any form or by any means,
without the prior written consent
of the publisher or a licence from
the Canadian Copyright Licensing
Agency (Access Copyright).
For a copyright licence, visit
www.accesscopyright.ca or call
toll-free to 1-800-893-5777.

Cataloguing data is available
from Library and Archives Canada
ISBN 978-1-77327-105-7 (hbk.)

Design by Rethink
Editing by Michael Leyne
Proofreading by Renate Preuss
Cover photograph by Clinton Hussey

Typeset in Tiempos Text and Circular
Printed on Rolland Opaque

Printed and bound in Canada
by Friesens
Distributed internationally
by Publishers Group West

Figure 1 Publishing Inc.
Vancouver BC Canada
figure1publishing.com

Figure 1
Vancouver / Berkeley

Rethink the Business of Creativity

Ian Grais,
Tom Shepansky,
Chris Staples

To all the Rethinkers and all the clients who believe.

Contents

Foreword	9
Introduction	13
PEOPLE	**18**
1. No Assholes	21
2. Rethink the Welcome	25
3. Space to Play	29
4. The Power of Appreciation	33
5. I Like, I Wish	35
6. No Group Briefs	39
7. Barges, Speedboats & Submarines	41
8. Shared Learning	45
9. Crowdsourcing	47
10. Never Fight a Battle Over Email	51
11. Friday Updates	53
12. WOOOing	57
13. Work-Life Balance	59
14. Irrational Celebration	63
15. Unskippables	65
16. Rethink Reviews	69
17. Founder Facetime	73
18. Congratulations to Us All	75
19. Coaching 101	79
20. Don't Fuck It Up	81

PRODUCT — 84

21. Find It, Steal It & Make It Your Own — 89
22. Listen & Learn — 91
23. The Shared Belief — 95
24. The Cocktail Party Test — 97
25. Traffic — 101
26. Office Hours — 105
27. Over-Overcommunicate — 107
28. How to Have an Idea — 111
29. Fast & Loose — 133
30. The 1-or-100 Rule — 139
31. Peer Review — 143
32. The Ping-Pong Ball Theory — 147
33. CRAFTS — 149
34. ACTS, Not Ads — 153
35. Shallow Holes — 161
36. The Deep Dive — 165
37. Dealing with Client Input — 167
38. If It's Wounded, Kill It — 171
39. KG — 173

PROFIT — 176

40. Believers Create Believers — 181
41. Output vs. Hours — 183
42. Cheap & Cheerful — 187
43. Astroturf — 189
44. Promote from Within — 193
45. Shared Leadership — 195
46. Flat Structure — 199
47. How to Share Profits — 201
48. No Us vs. Them — 205
49. DIY HR — 207
50. In-House Production — 213
51. R+D Days — 215
52. Change Proposals — 221
53. Cherish Independence — 229
54. The Long Game — 231
55. Rethinking Succession — 235

Shout-Outs — 238
Notes — 240
About Rethink — 248

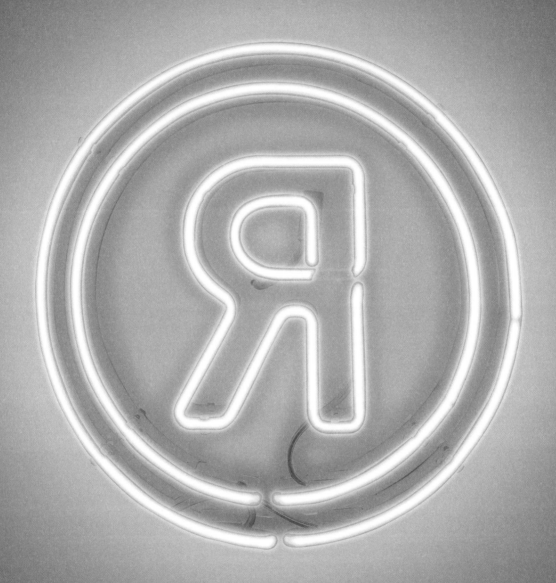

Foreword

When the three Rethink founders invited me to write this opening salvo, I was flattered but curious. "Why me?" I asked. "I've been out of the industry for nearly two decades!"

They answered: "Because you were smack in the middle of the West Coast creative renaissance that began fifty years ago. You showed up at historic moments. You rubbed elbows with the legends: Steve Jobs, Jay Chiat, Lee Clow, Frank Gehry... And you worked with high-tech pioneers like Intel, Apple, and Fairchild."

I've followed Chris, Tom, and Ian since they launched Rethink in 1999. They were competitors, but when they opened I became one of their biggest fans. I envied their talent, their enthusiasm, and their promise. They had the same restless spirit I had seen in creative greats up and down the West Coast. We'd stayed in touch. I enjoyed our chats.

Tom called in October. He, Chris, and Ian were in L.A., planning for their twentieth anniversary. He invited me over for a catch-up, just down the road from my place in Malibu.

Rethink was on quite a run: They'd blossomed to become Canada's top creative independent, with a level of creative output over the past twenty years that no other Canadian agency could touch. In two weeks they would be celebrated as the top digital agency in the country.

Back on their opening day, before the paint was dry, I gifted them a pricey bottle of Bookers to celebrate the birth. I told them to save it for "that landmark moment—you'll know it when it happens."

"Maybe tomorrow, when the electrician finally turns our power on," Ian groused.

The big moment occurred four years later, when *Marketing* magazine anointed them as Canada's Agency of the Year. They were throwing a celebration bash and Tom invited me. "We're cracking the Bookers and want to share it with you." The event was a love-in, packed with high-octane kids having fun. It reminded me of Chiat/Day and Goodby, Silverstein in their halcyon days—before they sold out to Omnicom.

We opened the booze in the stairwell while the party raged on. During a toast I implored them: "Don't ever sell!"

Rethink's mantra of People, Product, Profit places "people" as their centrepiece priority. They covet talented and enthusiastic ones who contribute to their special culture, and then incentivize them via imaginative policies and programs that you often don't find in typical ad firms. Like the advice offered in Work-Life Balance (p. 59): "Living at the office shouldn't be a point of pride." (Contrast that with the reputation of my alma mater, as exemplified by the office catchphrases "Chiat/Day and Night!" and "If you're not here on Sunday don't bother coming in Monday.")

Once an independent sells to a holding company, prioritizing people becomes impossible. Profit is number one. People become secondary: A means to an end. Expendable.

I know because I was pushed by my partners into selling to one.

Being independent, one could have a great financial year but make less the following year. Not so in the holding company world, where they might bonus you for that good year then assign you a target of 15 percent growth for the next—then punish you with staff cuts if you come up short.

Nothing destroys a creative culture as much as staff cuts. My first ad job was in L.A., with Chiat/Day. I was their first employee and spent twenty-three years there (including stints as founder CEO of their San Francisco and Toronto offices). We were the toast of the town. Then after Steve Jobs hired us at Apple, the toast of every town. But in our infancy we suffered a major setback when we lost our then-biggest account, Honda Automobiles. Honda was 60 percent of our revenue and 90 percent of our identity. It was demoralizing. The clinical decision would have been to immediately cut staff to adjust to the revenue shortfall.

But Jay Chiat wasn't clinical: "If we lose these people we've got nothing left. So if we're going to die, let's at least do it with drama."

The higher-paid people took 20 percent pay cuts, and everyone else took 10 percent. He held staff, dug in, and about six months later was able to restore everybody's salaries. Two months after that we all found envelopes on our desks. Inside was a cheque for the pay we had lost, with a one-word handwritten note from Jay: "Thanks."

Our competitors were doomed.

When Rethink began they reminded me of one of the West Coast's greatest creative companies ever: Goodby, Silverstein (to whom I lent a hand when they opened). Three charming, irresistible and talented guys escaping the purgatory of conglomerate agencies to create something unique. Goodby was the most electric shop in San Francisco. Once a year they threw a wild birthday party honoring Jeff Goodby's muse, Howard Gossage. Every creative lusted to work there. Nine years later the agency experienced some internal bickering. A partner left. They suffered some money angst. And they sold to Omnicom. Gossage parties became a thing of the past. Twenty years later, Jeff reflected on their decision: "If I look back on The Sale strictly from a financial standpoint, if I had to do it again, I'm not sure I would. I think we'd have made more money had we stayed independent."

The Rethink guys didn't make the same mistake.

When I reconnected with them in Malibu, I witnessed something reassuring and seldom seen: Nearly two decades later these guys had remained inseparable pals. Partners with shared values, a harmonic agenda, and an emboldened commitment to independence.

This degree of camaraderie is difficult to realize in long-term creative partnerships, especially in industries where egos frequently come into play, disagreements become irreconcilable, and selling looks like a way out.

It's a testament to Rethink's tenacity and passion that they forged a different path. They've stuck to their values and created something that just keeps getting better.

Enjoy and learn from this inspiring book. I certainly did.

Chuck Phillips
April 1, 2019, Malibu

Introduction

This is a book for creative problem-solvers. That means people in so-called "creative industries," like advertising, design, film, architecture, gaming, and software development. But it's also for anyone who wants to inject fresh creative thinking into their business, whatever that may be.

It's designed to be a tool kit of useful tips, tricks, processes, and beliefs that collectively can help create a culture that inspires great ideas, without sacrificing people's lives or the bottom line. These "tools" are the principles that we've retained as the industry and the world changes around us. They are the product of us continuously rethinking how we can create great work in a volatile business environment.

Each section is introduced by one of our founders and each chapter was created with contributions from Rethinkers across the country—both words and visuals. Feel free to read from start to finish, or jump around from chapter to chapter.

Some of the tools predate the founding of Rethink in 1999. In the early 1990s, Rethink's founders were working at an agency in Vancouver, hardly considered an advertising hot spot. Chris Staples and Ian Grais were creative directors, and Tom Shepansky was "the suit" in charge of accounts.

Palmer Jarvis was the biggest shop in town. They excelled at buying clients three-martini lunches, but very little else. This was borne out at the local awards show, where year after year PJ would win zippo. Finally, in 1993, owner Frank Palmer snapped. He had money, but no respect. He set out to change that by improving the agency's creative product. Frank brought in a retired ad guru named Ron Woodall to map out an exhaustive game plan with the audacious goal of reaching number one on the Canadian awards tally. It was a tall order for a shop then ranked sixty-ninth out of eighty-five. Three years later, Palmer Jarvis reached number one—and stayed there for years to come.

Several of the tools in this book were first implemented then, and were a big contributor to PJ's meteoric rise. Some of the tools came from Ian's experiences at ArtCenter, in Pasadena, then and now one of the most innovative ad and design schools anywhere. Others were borrowed from conferences like *Adweek*'s Creative Seminar, where we soaked up wisdom from advertising greats like Lee Clow and Jeff Goodby. Still others were created by our team, through hard trial-and-error.

The tools worked almost too well. In 1997, Frank sold his newly burnished agency to DDB, part of the Omnicom Group, both headquartered in New York. Despite assurances that nothing would change, everything soon did. Instead of worrying about consistent product, we started worrying about consistent profit. Even the photocopiers were modified so that you had to punch in a docket number to make a copy—all so every cent could be charged back to the client.

That was the genesis of Rethink—which was always intended to be a one-word business plan, both for us and our prospective clients.

What were we trying to rethink? First and foremost, the very definition of an "ad agency." By the late 1990s, many agencies had dealt with the changing ad world by creating divisions devoted to design or digital. These silos were pitted against each other, vying for their share of a client's budget. In our experience it was like kids fighting over a piece of pie, constantly kicking each other under the table.

We believed it was time for a new type of agency, one that embraced all forms of communications holistically. This meant that, instead of silos, Rethink would have one big creative department where designers and writers and art directors would sit side-by-side. As social media grew in importance, we added experts in digital and amplification to this model. Another key distinction was to have every Rethinker in every department working toward the goal of creating the best work of their careers— no matter if they were in creative, account services, or admin.

This holistic philosophy has allowed us to diversify our offerings far beyond those of most ad agencies, into brand planning, social strategy, and integrated design solutions. We still compete in the ad business, but we like to think we've evolved past just advertising. (Some Rethinkers hate even using the term "ad" or "agency" at all; when we use these terms in the following pages, know that we mean the new-and-improved kinds.)

The second thing we tried to rethink was the model that put profit before people and product. Omnicom talked about wanting to do great work and have a thriving culture, but the constant pressure to deliver 25 percent profit, quarter after quarter, made that a Herculean task. The result was fewer people working longer hours on more projects. It was still theoretically possible to do great work—but at a great cost to people's lives and happiness.

You'll notice that this book is divided into three sections: People, Product, and Profit. The order is very deliberate. We believe that if you create a culture that inspires and protects creative thinkers, they'll come up with better ideas. Especially when armed with processes that help ensure quality and efficiency every step of the way.

The end result is a creative product that gets talked about—which is the first job of any product, creative or otherwise. That in turn leads to better business results, which garner industry attention and accolades. All contribute to a strong bottom line—for the agency and its clients.

There's proof in Rethink's track record on all three measures, which have been remarkably consistent over the past twenty years (not to mention the long-term success of our clients, many of whom have been with us since the beginning). We measure how our people are doing with twice-yearly Culture Checks—simple surveys, with fewer than twenty questions, that cover things like overall happiness and work-life balance (our current blended score sits at an all-time high of 4.3 out of 5). On the product side, no agency in Canada has been more consistently celebrated for its creative output, year in and year out. Rethink has been in the top ten of Canada's awards rankings every year since 1999, including number-one titles five times. And when it comes to profit, we've never had a loss in twenty years, even during the financial crisis of 2008, when we rashly decided to proceed with plans to open an office in Toronto (followed shortly thereafter by Montreal).

Over the years, we've tweaked many of our original tools to better fit the realities of the digital world. That process continues, because to constantly evolve, reinvent, and challenge the status quo is what "rethinking" is all about.

Rethink founders from L to R: Ian Grais, Tom Shepansky, Chris Staples, 1999.
→

People

I always wanted to work in advertising, but I desperately wanted to avoid becoming an "ad guy." You know, like Darren Stephens on *Bewitched*. Working long hours, constantly entertaining clients, always at the whim of a mercurial boss. Martinis starting at lunch, switching to Canadian Club at the office long into the night.

Surely, I thought, you can do great work and still have a great life outside of advertising.

Sadly, advertising is like most creative industries in its cult-like celebration of the hard-core creative life. This seems to be defined as countless hours in search of the elusive "eureka" moment, followed by frenzied all-nighters and chaotic weekends before high-stakes presentations to demanding clients. Many of the most celebrated creative businesses almost seem to fetishize chaos and overtime as the only way to achieve greatness.

We call bullshit.

From day one at Rethink we've believed that if you put people first you'll get a better product, and a better business result for all involved. In short, you can win Cannes Lions and still be a great partner or parent.

In many creative industries, putting people first means things like having on-site cafes, gyms, and concierge services.

Perversely, all of these things are designed to entice people to stay at the office even longer. These kinds of cultures invariably lead to high rates of staff burnout. Comforts can mask chaos for only so long.

There are many other benefits to focusing on a people-first culture, including a lower turnover rate, in our case a third lower than the industry norm. By promoting from within and creating a supportive environment with ample opportunities, we hope to create a workplace that our people never want to leave. Judging by the large number of long-term Rethinkers, some of these policies and philosophies have borne fruit.

In the following section we'll outline some of the beliefs, policies, and processes we've used to help create a sustainable culture that promotes great ideas while protecting people's work-life balance. Some of these people-first practices are things we all learned in kindergarten but sometimes forget to practice in business: kindness, gratitude, and personal responsibility. Others are about creating a culture and workplace that inspire in ways large and small—through celebrating and sharing successes, and creating an environment that helps spark great ideas. Still others are about mentorship, of both people and ideas, so that both reach their full potential.

Like all of the tools in this book, some will apply to your situation better than others. Some are specific to the ad world, but most can be applied to any business. We hope you find them as useful as we have.

Chris Staples, Founding Partner

1 No Assholes

Creating a people-first culture means hiring only those who know how to play nice.

There are two secrets to running a creative business: hire the right people, and choose the right clients. In both cases, assholes are to be avoided at all costs.

That may sound like common sense. But it's surprising how many companies put up with assholes in their ranks, with the rationale that talent trumps niceness, that as long as someone is brilliant they can be excused for their appalling lack of social graces.

We beg to differ. Assholes are toxic and will corrode efficiency and productivity. If you're not careful, one asshole can single-handedly derail all three P's. They make the people around them unhappy, which shows through in the creative product, which leads to unhappy clients, loss of business, and reduced profit. Assholes are rarely worth it.

At Rethink, we protect ourselves from assholes by staying true to our values. When you look at every single decision you make through a people-first lens, you arm yourself against assholery right from the outset. If someone doesn't play nicely with others, it doesn't matter how talented they are, how many awards they've won, or how much money they make you.

Of course, the best way to avoid working with assholes is to not hire them in the first place. When we interview people, we trust the rule of first impressions: Within the first five minutes we ask ourselves, "Would I like to go for a drink with this person?" If the answer is no, the interview is usually over. In most creative industries if you don't make a good first impression, you probably won't get a chance to make a second.

On the client side, it's amazing how many creative businesses will put up with bad behaviour in order to win or keep a piece of business.

As in many creative industries, we win over prospective clients during a pitch process that often involves multiple meetings over a period of weeks. The client uses these meetings to whittle things down to a short list of one to three agencies. We use this process to ask ourselves whether we believe in the brand and the people behind it.

If there are assholes in the client ranks, we can generally suss them out. We've turned down major accounts because we knew that no matter the fees at stake, working for a bad client would cost us more in blood, sweat, and tears.

In the unfortunate event that an asshole does end up within your walls, it's important to act fast. Each day they stay is another opportunity for them to damage relationships, normalize bad behaviour, and drain morale. And keeping them around signals complacency on your part—by continuing to sign an asshole's paycheque, you're implicitly condoning their behaviour. Your other employees are bound to notice, and may question your commitment to your values. So sit the asshole down, tell them it's just not a good fit, and send them on their way (with a fair compensation package).

Life's too short to work with assholes.

ARE YOU AN ASSHOLE?

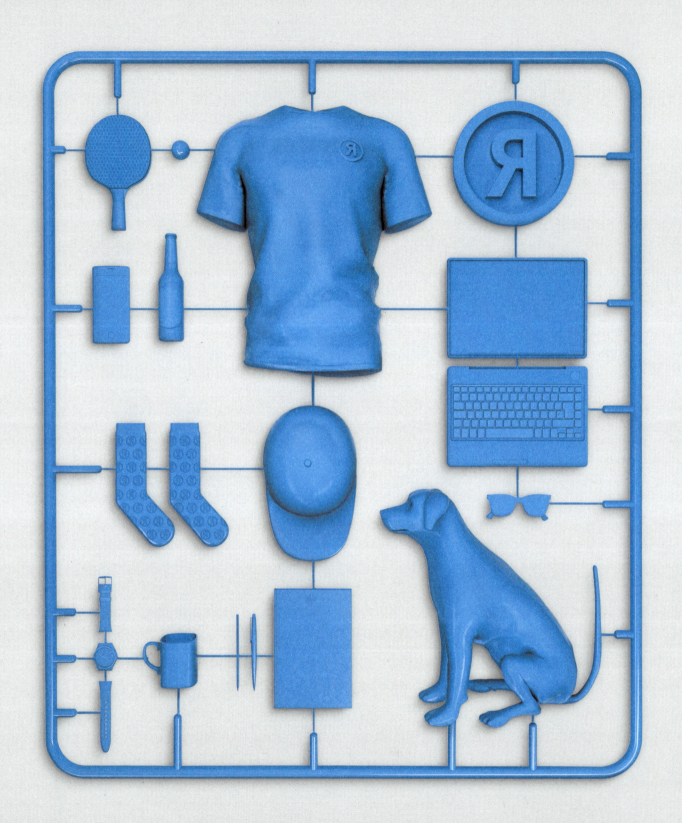

2 Rethink the Welcome

An office tour isn't enough. Help new employees hit the ground running with a thorough, self-guided orientation.

Why does employee orientation suck at most creative companies? It's partly the nature of creative businesses, which are usually a bit chaotic to begin with. But our sense is that most companies don't realize how stressful it is for people to start a new job—and how important it is that they feel welcome from the beginning.

New employees are eager and ready to learn. They're usually also nervous about proving themselves as quickly as possible. Luckily, new staff tend to have a light-ish workload, at least to start. It's up to you to take advantage of those early days so newcomers are primed for success. There are a few simple ways you can help people fit into your culture in those critical early weeks.

Learning and stress relief can begin even before an employee's first day. A week before the start date, we like to send them a Welcome Letter. It's designed to alleviate any stress or first-day jitters, provide a lay of the land, and give them their first assignment: to go for coffee (which they can expense, of course) with a different Rethinker every day of their first month.

Challenging your new employees to go for coffee with as many fellow co-workers as possible fast-tracks their integration into your culture. No manual can get a newbie up to speed as quickly or effectively as connecting face-to-face with co-workers from every department, including department heads. Think about it: for less than the cost of a cup of coffee per day, you can make a believer out of anyone.

Once an employee has toured the office and knows where the washrooms are, they're given a copy of the Survival Guide, something every company should have. Whereas the Welcome Letter is high-level, the Survival Guide gets into the nuts and bolts of the Rethink Machine (p. 87). It covers many of the tools outlined in this book, from Peer Review to The 1-or-100 Rule to Shallow Holes. In addition to outlining the processes we use, the Survival Guide is a useful deprogramming tool. It's thirteen pages of highly concentrated Rethink Kool-Aid for new staffers to ingest during their first week.

New hires from other companies tend to bring a fair amount of baggage with them. Many of them come from chaotic, free-flowing environments, and need to adapt to a more structured workplace that includes things like formal Office Hours (p. 105). And some of them come from shops owned by multinational holding companies—those people in particular need to learn to resist the urge to say, "At my old job…" We have a simple rule for new staff: Be open to learning new ways of doing things for the first six months. Learn our system inside and out. Then we'll be happy to hear your suggestions for improvements.

One handy way to help new employees climb the learning curve is to give them access to your archive of recorded Lunch 'n' Learns and all-staff meetings (see Shared Learning, p. 45).

Instead of sitting around waiting for the work to pick up, they can absorb a decade's worth of inspiration.

And finally, a vital point we convey to newcomers: We are a culture of joiners. We're highly social, like to have fun, and strongly encourage anyone new to throw themselves headlong into our culture. Staying for a beer on Fridays or joining a club or the Rethink Band is just as valuable as nailing an assignment. The best way to stick around at a people-first company is to connect with the people.

③ Space to Play

Ease work stress with a relaxed office environment inspired by play.

If our work was purely analytical, perhaps a sterile beige office filled with cubicles and fluorescent light would make sense. But we work in an industry where ideas are currency and the next creative idea could lead to more business. Our people are our product, so it's up to us to create optimal conditions for them to thrive.

Which brings us to the Rethink Lego Room.

The Lego Room is a meeting room that has two walls covered with those green Lego base plates, and a giant see-through box of Lego pieces in the middle of the room. On the walls are dozens of Lego creations in various stages of completion. We didn't make the room just because Lego is special to us (though it is). It's also a cheap and cheerful way to stimulate creativity while contributing to a more relaxed work environment.

While many companies praise workers for coming in at 7:00 AM and leaving at 8:00 PM, research is finding that overwork hurts creativity. Brigid Schulte, author of *Overwhelmed: Work, Love and Play When No One Has the Time*, says in an article for CNN headlined "Leisure Is the New Productivity" that "neuroscience is finding that when we are idle, in leisure, our brains are most active.... The 'a-ha' moment comes in a calm, relaxed state, when we are doing anything BUT work." What better way to foster "a-ha" moments than by creating a workspace that feels like a play area?

We don't stop at the Lego Room, either. Our entire office incorporates elements that feel whimsical and playful: Bright green Astroturf. Traffic cones as lighting fixtures. Brightly coloured maps, globes, and clocks. And, of course, the ultimate stress-relief tool—dogs.

On any given day there are bound to be a handful of canine co-workers at Rethink. Having an open-door policy for office dogs is obviously a massive perk for our employees who would otherwise have to deal with doggie daycare and make special arrangements for working overtime. But there's more to it than that: the presence of a dog has been scientifically proven to have a relaxing effect, diffusing the tension that can arise in any workplace (even one with Lego).[1] Many times we've heard clients remark, upon being greeted by an office dog, "I wish I worked at a place like this!" We pride ourselves on always being the highlight of our client's day. Yes, there's the occasional accident on the Astroturf, and shedding is certainly an issue, but the joy that dogs bring to the office outweighs the cost of the occasional steam cleaning.

Beer Cart Fridays are another great tool to promote relaxation and socialization. Every Friday afternoon at four, a pair of Rethinkers decorate the beer cart, fill it with an assortment of beverages (alcoholic and non-alcoholic), and push it around the office, delivering drinks to anyone who wants one. When everyone has their drink, Rethinkers congregate in a circle of comfy red IKEA chairs to enjoy the last few minutes of the week. As a result, rather than leaving at 4:55 PM, many people choose to stick around well past five to socialize.

With an open and relaxed attitude (and more than a few free drinks), we're able to make being at the office feel less like a chore. Anything we can do to stimulate people's right brains and squeeze out a few extra happy endorphins is certainly worth the investment.

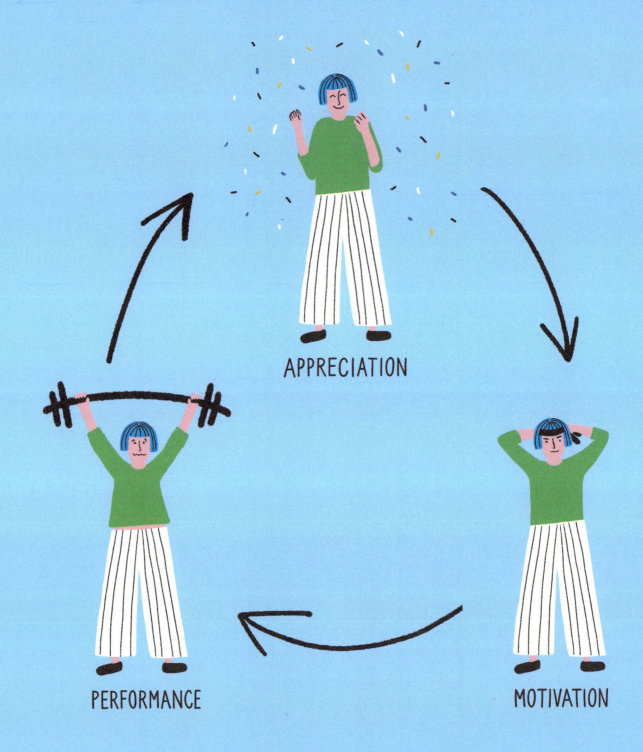

4 The Power of Appreciation

There are powerful links between appreciation, motivation, and performance. It all starts with gratitude.

It's human nature to seek approval, and this desire is likely even stronger for creative types. When they pour their hearts into something, they crave acknowledgement (no matter how it turns out), not just for their talent but for their effort. They want to be seen and validated. And if you can find ways to give them recognition, they'll repay you for it with even more effort. A staff that feels appreciated will be happier, work harder, and save you money by improving your retention rate.[2] (Rethink's retention rate, for example, is 30 percent higher than the average for our industry.)

Simply put: appreciate your employees, and they'll appreciate you back.

Appreciation can take many forms. When someone goes beyond the call of duty we like to reward them with an experience they can share with their long-suffering partner or spouse. A perfect example of this is the coveted Rethink Dinner. Instead of simply giving a monetary bonus, we like to give deserving people

$300 to spend at a restaurant of their choice. (The amount was chosen to make the thank-you seem special and talk-worthy.) These dinners get Rethinkers out on the town trying new things, make them feel appreciated, and even extend appreciation to their significant others and lucky friends who get to order the lobster.

Depending on the person in question, we've also offered spa days, sports tickets, and nights at boutique hotels. The more tailored to personal interests, the better. And of course, sometimes there's no better gesture you can offer than a much-needed day off.

That said, appreciation isn't all about grand gestures for huge accomplishments. It's important to notice and appreciate the little things with simple praise, in verbal or written form. Every single day, someone at your company does something worthy of recognition—so get in the habit of celebrating small victories. Did someone present their work clearly and articulately? Tell them. Did admin set up a complicated conference call? Say thank you. Make a point of making the rounds to people's desks, congratulating them on their completed projects and acknowledging their contributions. Speak loudly, so other people hear. And don't forget to submit your shout-outs for the Friday Update (p. 53). There's absolutely no reason whatsoever to be stingy with praise—it costs you nothing, but it can mean everything to the people you work with.

5 I Like, I Wish

Soften the blow of criticism by leading with something positive.

This one's a relatively simple hack for tactfully delivering criticism to creative people. In our business, this means creative directors giving feedback to writers, art directors, and designers.

Humans are inherently sensitive to criticism. For evolutionary reasons, we process criticism the same way we do a physical attack, which lights up the amygdala, the centre of our brain's emotional and decision-making processes, and triggers a fight-or-flight response.[3] Our instinctual response to criticism is to either get defensive and argue, or retreat inward and play it safe. Unfortunately, neither of these responses is particularly useful in an office environment. But we have a simple tool to help.

"I like, I wish" is how we give feedback in a way that's both constructive and protective. By starting with something you like, you keep the focus on what's working, and preserve your employee's sense of self worth. It works for just about everything:

- "I like the execution. I wish the concept was clearer."
- "I like the big thinking. I wish it was more achievable."
- "I like the insight. I wish the script was less metaphorical."

Instead of shooting down ideas, you're building on them. You're acknowledging that there's something there worth digging into further. You're encouraging exploration and problem solving, without attempting to solve it yourself (see Coaching 101, p. 79). Even if it seems like your creative staff have nothing, if you look hard enough, chances are there's some glimmer of hope you can focus on.

If you stick with this approach you'll eventually see a difference in your creative staff's confidence. When they believe in your ability to tease out the best parts of their ideas, they'll start bringing you more original thinking, more new ways to find a solution. They'll learn what you like, and what you don't, both of which will help hone their instincts. Instead of dreading feedback, they'll accept it as part of the creative process. And they'll internalize the fact that you want the exact same thing they do: great creative work on the table.

6   No Group Briefs

Don't assign multiple individuals or teams to solve the same creative problem. More people do not equal a better product.

Some companies like to throw a lot of people at their problems. When a big hairy project comes along, they set a false sense of security by thinking, "I've put all my top people on it!" This can mean multiple teams, or even the entire creative department, simultaneously working on the same brief. The bigger the problem, the more people who seem to be involved.

Although it's intuitive to think that directing more minds toward a problem will yield smarter solutions, we believe the opposite to be true. It causes "diffusion of responsibility," a psychological phenomenon in which every person involved assumes that someone else will solve the problem.[4] As you add to the mix, the more each individual's sense of responsibility is diluted. As a result, you might end up with four teams each giving 10 percent, instead of one team giving 110 percent. You may have more ideas to sift through, but they'll be underwhelming.

Even worse, group briefs pit your staff against one another, creating a toxic dynamic. Competing with other teams in the office causes unnecessary anxiety—not an ideal mindset for creativity—and leads to a "closed door" environment, where instead of openly sharing ideas through Peer Review (p. 143), teams will hesitate to reveal their precious ideas to any potential rivals. Competition can also lead to a sense of hopelessness if teams feel they don't have a decent shot at winning, in which case they'll be much less compelled to pour themselves into the work.

When you put a single team on a brief it allows them to own the project from the outset, which leads to a robust sense of responsibility for the final product. Without the safety net of other teams working on the same thing, they'll approach the problem from every conceivable angle, hunting for that special something that will dazzle the clients and their co-workers. Even if the results don't blow anyone's mind (but see Don't Fuck It Up, p. 81), the team will have something to show for their effort—and the next time they receive this magnitude of responsibility, you know they'll work even harder to create something they can be proud of.

The one-team-per-brief model also helps to conserve valuable resources. Why assign eight people to a job that two people could do better? When you trust your people to nail the brief they're assigned to, you free up other people to work on more briefs. You also get a more open, collaborative creative department where teams help each other and everyone shares the credit (see Congratulations to Us All, p. 75).

7 Barges, Speedboats & Submarines

Keep your people motivated with at least one hard-working project and one creative opportunity in the pipeline at all times.

In case you haven't realized it yet, we really do like our metaphors around here. And when talking internally about our clients, we prefer to use nautical ones. Our clients tend to fall into two categories: barges and speedboats.

A barge is typically a big retainer client. They want to do great work, but their size and the weight of decades-old habits make it hard to move forward, let alone steer in a new direction. Big barges tend to come with big budgets to match, but you can sure burn up a lot of fuel trying to move them.

Speedboats are way more nimble. The budgets are smaller but the projects move more quickly. They tend to have fewer levels of approval, so they're lighter and easier to steer. If you know what you're doing, a speedboat can be seriously fun. Just don't expect them to cover all your bills.

We believe that every creative staff member should divide their time between barges and speedboats. An employee who works only on barges is likely to burn out, stop trying, or abandon ship altogether. After a long day spent toiling on a barge, they deserve to take a speedboat out for a rip to blow off some creative steam. But if you give all the speedboats to a few "special" people, the barge hands will begin to resent them—and you.

There's a third type of ship we should include in this metaphor: submarines. We also call them Change Proposals (p. 221), or CPs. These are projects we agree to on a pro-bono basis, and often even invest in their production. CPs operate a lot like submarines, floating just below the surface of daily activity, waiting for the perfect moment to appear out of nowhere and blow up the internet. They're the passion projects, the cheap and cheerful not-for-profit ideas, the brilliant bombshells just waiting for a client who's daring enough to use them. If you ever feel like you don't have enough speedboat projects to go around, encourage your creatives to work on a change proposal and build themselves a submarine.

Of course, with barges, speedboats, and submarines, the right mix is crucial, both for individuals and Rethink as a whole. Barges pay the bills, but can be stressful. Speedboats and submarines may not pay the bills, but they pay off in happier staff and better creative output.

8 Shared Learning

If you want people to learn, make them teach.

In most industries, "on-the-job training" happens by osmosis—spend enough time working next to someone and you'll eventually pick up what you need to know. Unfortunately, the creative game changes so rapidly that there's no time to wait around for nature to take its course. Any business that isn't actively learning has already fallen behind. So if you really want to keep your people engaged and your company ahead of the curve, it's up to you to promote all kinds of shared learning.

A common approach to shared learning is the good old-fashioned Lunch 'n' Learn. Choose someone with wisdom to share, invite them to hold court, and provide a lunch for attendees. (Pizza always packs 'em in. Always.) And there's no need to limit the learning to only those able to get up from their desks and attend: thanks to modern technology, you can record your Lunch 'n' Learns for posterity (as we've done for years), creating a video archive that's easily accessible to all employees.

You needn't look outside your company for speakers. A lot of companies send employees to conferences or trade shows and then skip the critical step of having those employees report back. If you're going to pay to send someone across the country to sit in air-conditioned seminars, you might as well get your money's worth by having them share their findings with the whole office. This accomplishes two things: it spreads the conference knowledge to a wider audience, and it forces the "teacher" to really think about their key takeaways and put them in writing. Students memorize, but teachers internalize.[5] Once you teach something, you're more likely to remember it forever.

Shared learning doesn't have to be all pizza, PowerPoint, and professional development—you can also encourage more casual or extracurricular forms of learning: Send your staff to an improv workshop. Reimburse people for public-speaking lessons. Encourage employees to come up with their own activities by giving anyone the power to schedule an end-of-day event— we've hosted everything from book clubs to crochet lessons to terrarium-building lessons. (Note: we recommend doing these staff-selected initiatives at four in the afternoon on a Friday, the least productive hour of the week!)

9 Crowdsourcing

Good managers delegate.
Great managers crowdsource.

There's only so much of you to go around. If you own a business or are a senior manager, you probably feel overextended at least some of the time, which can make you shy away from new tasks. Good thing you have an office full of highly motivated individuals with a wide range of useful skills. By tapping into the time, resources, and skill sets of your whole workforce, you can unlock the full potential of your company.

Start by identifying and divvying up "low-risk" parts of the business that can be delegated. For example, planning the summer party might be a chore to you, but for the right up-and-comer or admin person it could be a fun project. Recurring meetings can have rotating chairpersons. The Friday Update (p. 53) can go to a different team each week, as can Beer Cart Friday duties (see Space to Play, p. 29). Even performance reviews can be shared among trusted partners.

Look for opportunities to shake people out of their usual roles. If you ask around the office, chances are you'll find all kinds of surprising resources that can save you time and money. Need to find music to play in the background of an event? Your co-worker with the massive vinyl collection probably knows the perfect record. You have musicians, voice talent, stylists, athletes, and artists in your midst, ready and willing to put up their hands. Send out an all-staff email and give them a chance. And be sure to show some love to those who step up (see The Power of Appreciation, p. 33).

Sharing the load like this isn't just efficient—it helps people grow. It brings out hidden strengths, lets everyone feel like they've contributed, and builds culture organically, from the bottom up. Simply put, crowdsourcing promotes an engaged workplace. Spread the load and reap the benefits.

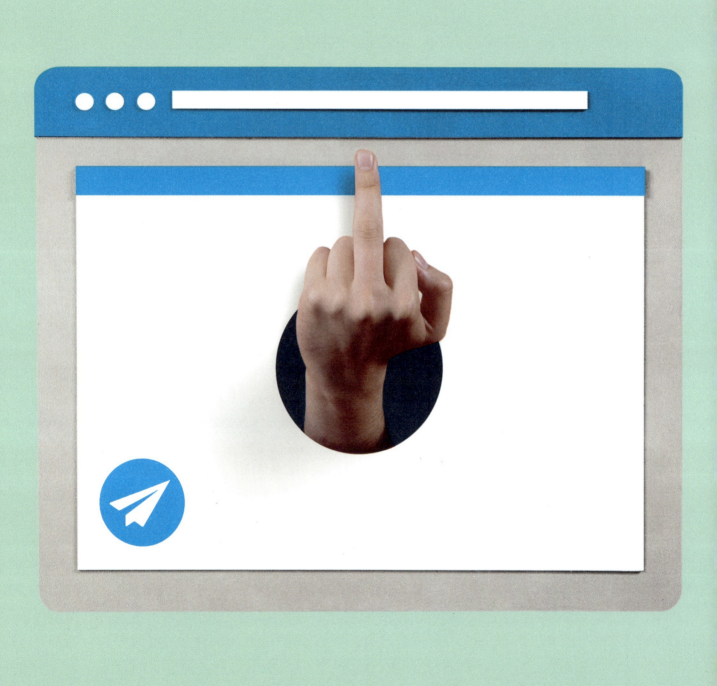

10 Never Fight a Battle Over Email

Email is impersonal. No amount of smiley-face emojis can change that.

Everyone knows the frustration that builds up when you get caught in an email battle. Each fresh email in the thread spikes your blood pressure as you dissect phrases and search for hidden meanings. You forget that you're sending words to a human and feel like you're fighting with a machine.

The problem is that facial expressions, tone of voice, and body language are all missing from email, which leads to increased anxiety and confusion for all parties.[6] Without these contextual cues, something as innocent as ending a sentence with a period instead of an exclamation point or smiley face can feel abrupt. This leads to senders walking on eggshells and recipients taking things the wrong way.

Interestingly, when you open an email you don't naturally read it from start to finish. Research shows that before your brain even processes its contents, your eyes scan it for threatening signs or key phrases.[7] In that instant, a large block of text or a negative phrase can feel like a threat, and trigger a fight or flight response much like the one we experience when confronted with criticism (see I Like, I Wish, p. 35). Before you've even read the email, you're primed to either ignore it or react to it negatively.

For all of these reasons, when email battles do arise and tensions start to get high, we like to pump the brakes, stop trying to read between the lines, and instead speak face-to-face. If you can't physically get everyone into the same room, get everyone on a call—ideally a video conference.

Despite email being touted as an efficiency tool, you'll find that turning digital confrontation into human collaboration will actually make you more efficient. In less time than it would take to compose the perfect reply, you can easily pick up the phone and work toward a solution.

This isn't to say that you should ditch email entirely—it's still a useful tool for day-to-day conversation (although better digital tools, like Vancouver's own Slack, are on the rise). But use it wisely, know its shortcomings, and learn to recognize when it's time to take things offline.

Friday Updates

Every week, send an office-wide email with both project updates and crowdsourced shout-outs.

You would think that companies in the business of communication would be great internal communicators. In our experience that's rarely the case. At many agencies, the first time most folks see new work is during a commercial break, or while they're whizzing past a billboard.

At Rethink, an all-staff email goes out every Friday containing updates on clients, on business in general, and on the work everyone's doing. And it includes a whole long list of anonymous "shout-outs," which are Rethinkers congratulating Rethinkers on a job well done.

Shout-outs are the secret sauce in every Friday Update. They're anonymous, easy to write, and can be given for any achievement, large or small, so everyone can feel recognized. Some come in the form of a video, some are punctuated with fun GIFs, some have a creative theme, and some are just straight text. But no matter the format, they're something everyone looks forward to.

Sending a shout-out to someone who deserves it feels just as good as receiving one, and peer-to-peer recognition has been shown to be just as important as recognition from the top.[8]

With over a hundred shout-outs in a typical week at Rethink, there's also a cumulative effect: when you scroll through a seemingly endless outpouring of love and appreciation among your peers, you're bound to feel all warm and fuzzy.

Friday Updates don't have to be a big commitment, because the entire process can be crowdsourced (see Crowdsourcing, p. 47). The task of sending it at Rethink rotates among twenty or so partners, but the content itself comes from the staff. Throughout the week, staff send email updates and shout-outs to the partner in charge, who simply collects that content, formats it, and sends it out on Friday afternoon. This lessens the burden on management and lets everyone contribute to the Friday Update—and when you've contributed to something you're more likely to actually read it.

The Friday Update might not seem like a big deal, but it's so much more than a weekly all-staff email. It promotes radical transparency by giving everyone a bird's-eye view of what's going on across all offices. It can be inspiring to see just how much is being accomplished in other departments. And it's a simple and fun way to personally engage and celebrate the achievements of your staff, which fosters a better culture and keeps people happy. In a creative field that can often leave people fatigued, nothing could be more important.

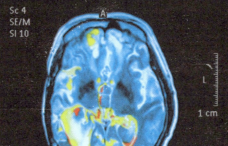

Brainstorming in a cubicle.

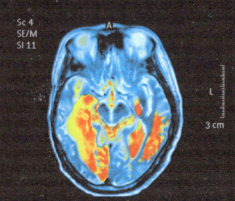

Brainstorming in a coffee shop.

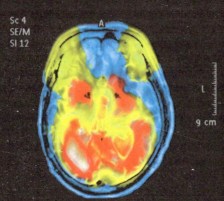

Brainstorming on a nude beach.

12 WOOOing

Let your staff work at the time and place that's best for them.

Everyone has their own perfect scenario to get the creative juices flowing, and few of them involve a cubicle or an office. More and more companies are exploring flexible work arrangements, because even the most thoughtfully designed offices are full of distractions (people, dogs, meetings, free donuts, etc.), and low on inspirational stimuli. Our brains thrive on stimuli—the greater the variety of input, the better the output.[9] To tap the full potential of your creative minds, let them out into the world.

We call this WOOOing (Working Out Of Office). We do it not to provide staff with a perk, but because greater freedom means greater creative output. An employee who is entrusted with freedom will feel obligated to deliver on that trust by producing great work.

A WOOO policy makes sense because people have different schedules for optimal performance. Some jump out of bed and hit the ground running. Others start by sipping coffee and browsing social media (not that there's anything wrong with that!), then gain steam throughout the day. Many creative people find that they fritter away their days at the office, unable to focus, then get the bulk of their work done after hours. If you force someone to work when they're sub-optimal, you'll get sub-optimal work. But WOOOing lets everyone work in their prime time and place, yielding maximum productivity.

Allowing your staff to WOOO certainly empowers them—but with great power comes great responsibility. For the system to work, everyone must be held personally responsible for getting their to-do list done, even if how they do it is up to them. Staff must also be responsible for communicating their whereabouts, checking in with their teams as needed, and being reachable in case of an emergency. They still have to come into the office for certain meetings and client presentations, but beyond that, why micromanage?

Let's be honest: people will find excuses to be out of the office anyway. They have dentist appointments, childcare issues, cars to maintain, tradespeople to wait for… Sure, you could try to keep tabs on everyone's coming and goings, but is that really how you want to spend your precious time? Some companies opt for job sharing or flex time to give people space for their personal errands and obligations, but we've found these approaches to be problematic, particularly in a client service industry that requires 24/7 availability.

WOOOing provides much-needed flexibility, but not at the expense of access. If you truly believe in your people, it's in your best interest to let them WOOO.

13 Work-Life Balance

Creativity comes from living. If your people don't have time to lead a good life, they won't do good work.

Too often, creative types wear their late nights and weekends at the office as a badge of honour. They proudly rattle off the number of overtime hours they've worked as though it's a testament to their dedication.

But living at the office shouldn't be a point of pride, particularly for people who are paid to make relatable insights. How can anyone hope to be relatable if they spend eighty hours a week in the same chair, talking to the same people, who work in the same industry? By focusing on three key areas, we've built a culture that values work-life balance.

It starts with enforcing regular, uninterrupted holidays for all staff. Offering three weeks of paid vacation even to entry level employees—and then making sure they can actually take those days off—sends the message that recharging is an important part of the creative process. Staff should never be encouraged to take calls, check email, or otherwise be available on their holidays, as this defeats the purpose of unplugging in the first place. Management should strive to lead by example—even owners and founders should be unreachable when on vacation. Work schedules will occasionally need to be rejigged to fit around vacation schedules (see Traffic, p. 101).

This next point might be controversial, particularly among the younger generation, who are accustomed to constant connection: we've found that disabling one's work email during non-work hours is incredibly beneficial for mental well-being, and can help avoid burnout. The deluge of email in the morning is more than worth it to escape the intermittent buzzing and beeping that can keep you awake at night. The more you force yourself to disengage, the more engaged you'll be when you come back online. If something's ever truly an emergency (which it rarely is), a text message can reach someone in a pinch. Just be sure to make that the exception, not the rule.

Finally, we help foster balance by reducing chaos during working hours. In the next section, Product, we'll cover a raft of policies, from Office Hours (p. 105) to routinized Over-Overcommunication (p. 107), that mean fewer late nights and weekends for all.

You might think that less overtime would lead to less output. It's counterintuitive, but better work-life balance has actually been shown to improve productivity.[10] Once your staff accepts that working late isn't a virtue, and that when you tell them to leave the office it isn't some sort of trick, you can expect to see an uptick in nine-to-five productivity. Employees will begin to work smarter, not longer, because they have exciting non-work things to look forward to.

And when they're not at the office, they'll find ways to feed their inner artist. They'll go to shows, concerts, and galleries; they'll try new restaurants, take classes, work on side projects—and then they'll have exponentially more material to draw inspiration from. As the quality of their life improves, so will the quality of their ideas.

 slide to power off

- LOAF DAY
- TREAT YO'SELF DAY
- We ♥ hearts
- SALUTE TO BEER
- Happy 200th of June
- WHY NOT?
- WHAT THE FRIDAY
- Good Luck, Person Who Quit!
- JUST CUZ

14 Irrational Celebration

The right mix of celebrations—traditional or spontaneous, mellow or over-the-top—will help you build a culture people want to participate in.

At a busy workplace with tight deadlines, taking the time to celebrate together can start to feel like a chore. If you don't want your employees just going through the motions, showing up for "mandatory fun time," you need to take a fresh approach. At Rethink, we've consciously decided over the years to foster a culture of irrational celebration. We strive to facilitate fun moments that people will want to opt in to, rather than try to get out of.

Several times a year we hold Rethink Afternoons, when we close the office early to go do an activity like lawn bowling or a scavenger hunt. We've had chili cook-offs, sports days, and dog shows. And every year we go all-in on Valentine's Day, with a hearts tournament, a secret Valentine competition, and an office-wide outpouring of love.

Don't feel like you need to wait for an official holiday to have a party. Instead, look for creative excuses to celebrate. Just got a major campaign approved? Bring in champagne and charcuterie. Win an important piece of new business? Send the whole staff on a school bus to an amusement park.

If done right, celebrations can rally people, strengthen team bonds, and even empower staff to find new reasons to celebrate. For example, one Rethinker invented a new holiday, The 200th of June, as an excuse to go out for a boozy lunch on December 17. Today, The 200th of June is an annual event with its own elaborate customs and traditions, such as giving stolen gifts and feeding your neighbour a bite of your food. All management does is chip in for a round of drinks. Often the events that arise organically are the ones that become the most treasured.

We even celebrate people on their way out—every staffer who leaves gets a party featuring the Rethink Band. Remember, the goal of all of this is to give your staff those special moments they'll look back on someday and say, "Remember the time when…?"

These are the kinds of moments they'll tell their friends about—moments that will earn your company a lasting reputation as a unique, fun place to work. A place where people are empowered to do wacky new things with their co-workers and friends… who wouldn't want to work there?

15 Unskippables

Not all meetings are a waste of time. Identify the key ones, and make them mandatory.

At many creative companies, hectic schedules cause regularly scheduled meetings to fall to the wayside. It's no wonder people complain about a lack of communication! The right kind of meetings can make all the difference when it comes to generating shared vision—and profit.

It starts out innocently enough—a meeting gets pushed a day here, a week there; or maybe one meeting is skipped because no one can make it—but it's a slippery slope that can lead to no key meetings at all. Which in turn leads to lack of alignment and inefficiency.

When we say a meeting is "unskippable," we mean it. For big unskippable meetings we'll have Traffic (p. 101) book two separate hold times into everyone's calendars, sometimes months in advance, just to ensure that everyone can attend. We do this for a variety of meetings, from monthly Creative Director Calls to quarterly Partner Meetings. Even if a meeting turns out to be just a fifteen minute check-in, just the act of having the meeting keeps our various departments and multiple offices on the same page.

Perhaps the most sacred and unskippable meeting of all is the Creative Meeting. Every six weeks we convene the entire creative department, across all three offices, for three hours. There are no excuses for not attending—client presentations and video shoots are booked around the Creative Meeting, not the other way around. During the meeting, each creative team in turn shares their latest work via Skype, along with any useful insights they picked up along the way (see Shared Learning, p. 45).

We're obsessive about keeping the Creative Meeting unskippable because it's one of our most inspirational and motivational tools. It's rewarding for teams to showcase work they're proud of. When work really stands out, the applause in the room speaks for itself. And nothing lights a fire under your ass like seeing other people being lavished with praise for amazing work. Creative Meetings help us keep our product bar high. If a team ever has nothing to share in a Creative Meeting, they should be worried.

We're also particularly stubborn about annual reviews (see Rethink Reviews, p. 69). Reviews are some of the most meaningful conversations of the year, but they're also easy to postpone or reschedule. When you make regular performance reviews a priority, you send a message that you value your people and care about their goals. If we ever have to postpone a review for any reason, we ensure that any salary adjustment is prorated back to the original review date.

Don't get us wrong—we don't want to sit in meetings all day. But by choosing a few important ones to commit to, you avoid a plunge into chaos.

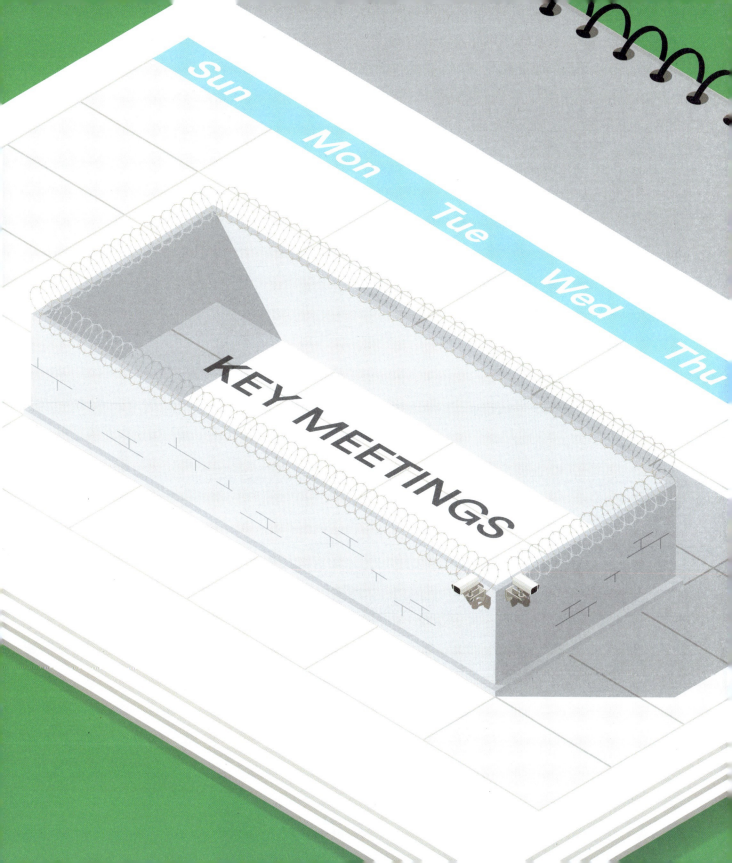

Three things I do well:

1
___
___

2
___
___

3
___
___

Three things I could work on:

1
___
___

2
___
___

3
___
___

16 Rethink Reviews

A performance review should never be a monologue delivered from on high. The best reviews are crowdsourced, constructive conversations.

Employee reviews have a tendency to fall to the bottom of the to-do list. It's easy to see why, really. The preparation takes time, and there's no apparent urgency. It's easy to find reasons to put them off, especially if you anticipate a tough conversation.

But if you're serious about being a people-first organization, you should make annual reviews a priority—and ensure the review process isn't too onerous for the reviewer or reviewee. No manager relishes the task of writing thousand-word essays on their staff.

The first way you can demonstrate the importance of reviews is by rigidly sticking to the review schedule (see Unskippables, p. 65). If a review gets pushed a week it can just as easily get pushed a month, and you want to avoid that slippery slope. Make them an absolute priority. Ideally, do them annually on an employee's exact start date, and set a reminder to start collecting feedback about a month before the actual review date.

When gathering feedback, be sure to talk to lots of different people across all departments, not just the one your reviewee works in. This crowdsourced approach will give you a better sense of where the employee stands both personally and professionally. If you don't get enough responses, make a point of personally contacting key people.

This doesn't have to be labour-intensive. We use an online form, but an envelope full of anonymous printouts would work just as well. And you only really need to ask two key questions: what are at least three of the reviewee's strengths, and what are at least three areas for improvement?

Once you have a sufficient pool of feedback, identify a few overarching themes for both strengths and weaknesses. Do this prior to the actual review. Generally, if you hear a certain comment from only one person it's not worth mentioning, but if three or more people say the same thing, that's a theme worth talking about. Pull quotes from the feedback to read aloud to the reviewee—but keep them anonymous. If colleagues know their feedback is anonymous, they're far more likely to be honest.

Book more time than you need for these meetings—a review should never feel rushed. When you're in the room with the reviewee, start by having them review themselves. What are they most proud of? What do they want to focus on in the year ahead? If an employee knows that they'll be kicking things off, they'll be more likely to come prepared. Often, they'll prove to be very self-aware of their perceived weaknesses, which makes things easier to talk about. Allow plenty of time for discussion, and as much as possible, try to let the reviewee lead the conversation. Allowing them to set the tone will give you valuable insight into their mindset, and will help them brush off any nervousness they might feel going into the review.

When the time is right, get into the verbal feedback. Remember to start with the good (see I Like, I Wish, p. 35). Then get into potential areas for improvement (which you'll hopefully have already touched on in the employee's self-assessment). If there's a salary adjustment or title change on the table, save that for the very end or it'll be all the reviewee can think about and they won't remember a word you say.

Nobody should ever be shocked by the feedback in a performance review, but if they are, come up with a plan of attack and schedule a follow-up. Ideally, the reviewee should leave the room feeling that they were heard, and knowing exactly where they stand and what needs to be done. You can sum up the review in an email with a few key bullet-points, which can be a valuable thing to check at next year's review.

Finally, remember that annual reviews should be just one of many touchpoints with your people. Don't wait until someone's review to bring up an issue—provide running feedback throughout the year.

Greg Kensmith

CEO

17 Founder Facetime

Your knowledge and your time are your most valuable resources—give more of them to your people.

Meaningful mentorship is a major gap at most companies. We know this because we hear it from new Rethink hires all the time. Many companies talk the talk, but few actually commit to providing mentorship opportunities, and fewer still think creatively about how to do it.

This is especially true in companies where the founders are still part of the day-to-day business. Founders are generally knowledge-rich but time-poor. To a junior employee, they might appear as blurry figures, only seen darting for the elevator. Mentorship is often reserved for a few select individuals, which can create a sense among employees that leadership is "picking favourites."

That's where Founder Facetime comes in—it's a system that makes mentorship democratic. It's not the only way we provide mentorship at Rethink, but it's an important foundation. In the Founder Facetime model, anyone in the organization can access direct mentorship from the owners of the company, or, if your company doesn't have founders or owners present, from the senior leadership team. The founders commit a certain chunk of their time (say, one or two days each quarter) to thirty-minute one-on-one mentorship sessions. Staff members can choose a founder and book a session, in person or via Skype, to ask questions, share concerns, seek advice, and generally learn directly from the leaders of their organization.

Staff are encouraged to be proactive and bring a topic of discussion to each session. This makes for an efficient use of time—and the founders can see who's interested, and what they're interested in. Sometimes the focus is on tips for generating ideas, or learning how to present those ideas more effectively. Other times the subject is long-term career goals and how to achieve them.

We try to be ruthless about protecting these sessions. Because in the end, meaningful mentorship isn't brain surgery. It's simply a matter of showing up.

18 Congratulations to Us All

Everyone gets credit—end of story.

No business congratulates itself more often than advertising. Awards matter, both for building buzz and attracting creative talent. They are often viewed as a measure of individual success, or one team's success, or the creative department's success. But, as with any corporate achievement, the credit needs to be spread around.

After major awards shows, we send out an all-staff email tallying up our haul and listing the projects that won. Pretty standard—except that we make a point of always including the same four magic words at the end of every one of these emails: "Congratulations to us all."

It's common to attribute the success of a creative endeavour to the person or team that led the charge, but we believe this view is misguided. We're playing a team sport and everyone deserves credit for a job well done. Saying "Congratulations to us all" reminds the creative teams that they have a whole support system working every day to bring their ideas to life, and it acknowledges that every single Rethinker, from accounting to admin to IT, shares responsibility for every shiny object we win.

And speaking of shiny objects... we don't display our awards. Instead, we give them to our clients, in recognition of the fact that we couldn't win without them. Behind every award-winning idea is a believer in the power of great creative—a client who was willing to sign off on it. Those trophies work harder for us sitting on our clients' mantles than they would gathering dust in our office. They make the client look good to their peers, and solidify our relationship.

LEADERSHIP ESSENTIALS

COACH'S WHISTLE

▸ Gives inspiring direction
▸ Champions great ideas
▸ Supports from a distance

— NOW —
99% EGO-FREE

19 Coaching 101

The first rule for creative coaches is to know when to get off the ice.

We like to think of Rethink's leaders as hockey coaches (we are Canadian, after all). A great coach can inspire their team, rallying everyone together under a single shared vision. A great coach can prepare and guide their team, by running drills, picking lines, and giving clear feedback. But the one thing even a great coach never, ever gets to do is skate out there, grab the puck, and try to score a goal themselves.

For creative leaders, the temptation is always there: The urge to do it yourself. To save the day and be the brilliant, last-minute hero. After all, having great ideas is what got you to where you are. Sometimes it seems easier to solve a problem yourself than to guide creatives to the solution. But if you do that, nobody learns or grows. Make it your personal goal to pull others up to your level, not push them down.

Leaders who hog the puck are often perceived as egotistical, and their subordinates tend to feel overlooked or ignored. There's nothing more demoralizing than working long, hard hours on a problem only to have it stripped away from you. It leads to grumbling, office politics, and, ultimately, people leaving.

By clearly defining the roles and limitations of leadership, companies can protect themselves from this toxic atmosphere. A creative leader can champion an idea by getting behind it and helping to sell it through, internally and externally. They can support an idea by offering wisdom, guidance, and suggestions. Or they can stay on the bench, and trust in their team to find a way to win.

One helpful tip for coaches: rather than drawing up detailed, thorough plans for success, try giving your team deliberately bad ideas. In our case, this means giving teams an example of a "bad ad"—a concept that hits the mark strategically, but has a corny or clichéd premise. This is a non-threatening way to make your point and nudge the team forward. It allows them to build on the momentum of the strategic truth, and turn your bad ad into something good.

When your team wins as a team, everyone keeps growing (see Congratulations to Us All, p. 75). So if you find yourself in a creative leadership position, don't let your ego or title get in the way of great ideas. Be secure enough in yourself to allow others to succeed, and recognize that respect comes from setting your entire staff up for success—not from putting your stamp on an idea just because you can.

20 Don't Fuck It Up

A not-so-gentle reminder for people taking direction and giving it—quality counts.

Like in most industries, creative businesses have a hierarchy. The shorts and sneakers and office dogs may create a casual vibe, but ideas still need to be generated, finessed, and approved. The bar is high, and so too is the pressure and responsibility.

In the ad business, it all starts with a client brief, then writers, designers, and art directors show their ideas to creative directors. Rough scribbles become finished ideas over the course of weeks or months, with lots of Office Hours sessions (p. 105) along the way. (Lots and lots and lots…) Many of our creative directors end each session with a simple instruction: don't fuck it up.

It always gets a laugh, usually a nervous one. And that's not such a bad thing. DFIU, as it's known internally, works two ways: It reminds people that sure, this is a fun place to work, but expectations are high. And it's a reminder to our CDs that teams can only succeed with clear, actionable direction.

In short, creative directors need to remember to *direct*. You'd be surprised how many CDs forget this basic rule. Their feedback will be some variation of "we're not there yet. Keep working. I'll know it when I see it."

For our CDs, DFIU acts like a checklist for every feedback session:

- **Direction**: Clarify the creative and strategic approach.
- **Feedback**: Tell the team what's working, what's not working, and why.
- **Instruction and Inspiration**: Give the team clear priorities on what to do next.
- **Understanding**: Help the team understand specific challenges and opportunities.

All of this takes time. It can't happen in an impromptu meeting in the hallway. It's far better when it's in person, rather than via text, phone, or email. It's your chance as a creative leader to really lead: To inspire and mentor. To be the kind of boss you wish you had.

To not fuck it up.

Product

At Rethink we've always thought of ourselves as creative problem-solvers, creating our own destiny. Through all that we've learned we've come to realize that the most important problem we've solved for ourselves has been how to solve problems. This includes all of the methods we use to create the strategy, content, and experiences that make up our product.

We've learned over the years that if you take care of your people (see the first section, People, p. 18) a healthy culture will grow, word will spread, and you'll attract the best creatives in your industry. But building a great team is not enough. You need a structure in place to set them up for success. You need to give them constant direction. And when something doesn't work out as planned, you need to course-correct and start again.

We learned the power of demystifying the process so that agency and client understand each other, and the creative people can relax and flourish.

We learned that creativity grows when it's shared in a spirit of collaboration, not locked away and guarded as the domain of one team or department.

But mostly we learned not to be scared of order and discipline—these things actually set you free. They create protected spaces that allow teams to soar. Order allows more time for courageous, provocative creative thinking.

If this sounds a bit controlling, it probably is. From our early days creating a strong creative culture at Palmer Jarvis we realized that a dose of discipline goes a long way and that something magical happens if we grow up and stop acting like the creative "children" in the agency, with the account people being the "parents." Management takes you seriously, and so do your clients. And once this happens the organizational imperative shifts away from blindly pleasing your clients at all costs, and people awaken to the potential of creative insights, ideas, and executions, and their power to solve real problems and inspire change.

We felt this shift at Palmer Jarvis during the 1990s. Then, when DDB took over, priorities changed and we felt the drag of profit trumping people and product. That inspired us to venture down our own path, one where we could rethink each and every day.

We started by examining how people usually generate ideas in our industry, which can be chaotic to say the least. So we built a platform for creative problem-solving that is customized for us and our clients, but is scalable and transferrable to new offices, new clients, and new cultures. And it's more sustainable in the long run, because it removes common barriers and friction points for creativity, thus protecting teams from burnout.

We like to think we've come up with some useful ways to protect and encourage creativity, and to produce better work more easily and efficiently. We're especially proud of taking these solutions and codifying, designing, and packaging them in this book so they're memorable and portable. This makes them "sticky." It also keeps us from repeating and reinventing the same processes over and over again.

Along the way we've experienced huge industry change as the internet has affected every part of our business: Tools and channels have become available to everyone. Data and digital experiences impact how people act. Attention has become more fleeting and thus even more valuable.

Through all this change we've realized that some things are timeless: a memorable story, an elegant design solution, a powerful human insight, an infectious new idea. We returned again and again to tools and processes that remained relevant. And we rethought new ones.

Eventually we had a collection that we started calling "The Rethink Machine." Its parts collectively define our creative principles and process. The Machine is the result of twenty years of trial-and-error. We think it has broad applications beyond advertising and design, to any industry that values ideas or needs to create them.

Feel free to take it for a test drive. We hope what works for us will help inspire greatness for you.

Ian Grais, Founding Partner

- STRUNK AND WHITE — THE ELEMENTS OF STYLE
- Tribes — SETH GODIN
- LATERAL THINKING — EDWARD DE BONO
- Jean-Marie Dru — La publicité autrement
- blink — The Power of Thinking Without Thinking — Malcolm Gladwell — Little, Brown
- Hey Whipple, Squeeze This — The Classic Guide to Creating Great Ads — FIFTH EDITION — SULLIVAN BOCHES
- CONSCIOUS CAPITALISM — MACKEY SISODIA — Harvard Business Review Press
- Les 36 cordes sensibles des Québécois — Jacques BOUCHARD
- A SMILE IN THE MIND — Beryl McAlhone, David Stuart
- TO STEAL IS GENIUS — ONE SHOW
- BILL BERNBACH'S BOOK — BOB LEVENSON

# 21 Find It, Steal It & Make It Your Own

Get inspired by the best—
and don't be afraid to shoplift.

One of the hallmarks of great creative thinkers is curiosity. It's also one of the driving forces behind the Rethink brand—you can't rethink things without getting inspiration from somewhere.

Sadly, the type of "professional development" that most creative industries practice is rarely inspiring. The ad business, for instance, has dozens of awards shows. These self-congratulatory gatherings are a great way to catch up with friends and keep tabs on enemies, but rarely a source of true inspiration. Most of the work, after all, is months or even years old.

A few awards shows have tried to add more value by hosting conferences before or after the ceremonies. This is where we've put our professional development focus over the years. These conferences, as in most creative industries, are simply a chance to see and hear successful people tell their stories. And what inspiring stories they are! We've heard the creators of the Got Milk? campaign talk about how studying people in their homes sparked this amazing insight. We've heard the brains behind French Connection talk about how they fcuk-ed the fashion industry. We've heard many of the creative greats of the last quarter century from our industry and beyond.

And we've stolen something great from every single one of them.

Some of our most famous Rethink philosophies were inspired by others. For instance, the Ping-Pong Ball Theory (p. 147) came from a presentation we saw by Graham Page about the need for simple, clear messaging[11]—although the speakers didn't use the analogy of Ping-Pong balls. We added that metaphor because in our experience, ideas become popular when they've got a catchy name or a memorable metaphor.

We make a point to send people from different departments to various conferences, even if the focus is on the creative side of the business. Their job is to listen and learn, and then come home with their top ten takeaways, which they share with everyone at a Lunch 'n' Learn session (see Shared Learning, p. 45).

We experiment with new ideas and tools by first trying them out on small projects in a single office. The ones that work are shared across the company. In this way, the Rethink Machine—stolen parts and all—continues to run at top speed and efficiency.

If you find something useful in this book, steal it. Maybe one day we'll return the favour.

㉒ Listen & Learn

Learn *from* people, not just about them.

Many creative industries are a mix of art and science. An architect won't get too far if shoddy engineering makes their beautiful buildings fall down. But in marketing, people sometimes try to use scientific principles at the strategic stage of the process, to help decide who to talk to and what to say to them. They rely on cutting-edge research models to provide insight. The most extreme methods involve hooking up sensors to people's brains and following their eye movement.

We prefer chatting instead.

Authenticity comes directly from people's mouths, not from sensors. It's easy to stay at arm's length and draw correlations from data… but data in a vacuum can be dangerous and misleading.[12] Learning about people happens at a distance, whereas learning from people requires proximity.

We learn better by doing the legwork, extracting the stories that support the data. We approach research like journalists do:

we start with the readily available facts, then validate them by talking to actual people who are involved in what we're interested in. If we're trying to reach busy moms, for example, we'll tag along with moms to a hockey practice. Advertising is a form of storytelling, after all. If our output is stories, shouldn't our input be stories, too?

If we want to tell someone a story that they'll believe (and that will cause them to change their behaviour), we have to draw from real experiences from real people. One-on-one conversations beat focus groups every time. Putting consumers behind glass and serving them stale sandwiches is a recipe for group-think and disaster.

Even the very concept of learning from "consumers" is flawed. People are people, not simply gaping voids ready to mindlessly consume products and messages. Remembering this simple fact makes all the difference, whether in crafting strategies or finished campaigns.

The human touch makes all the difference in the world.

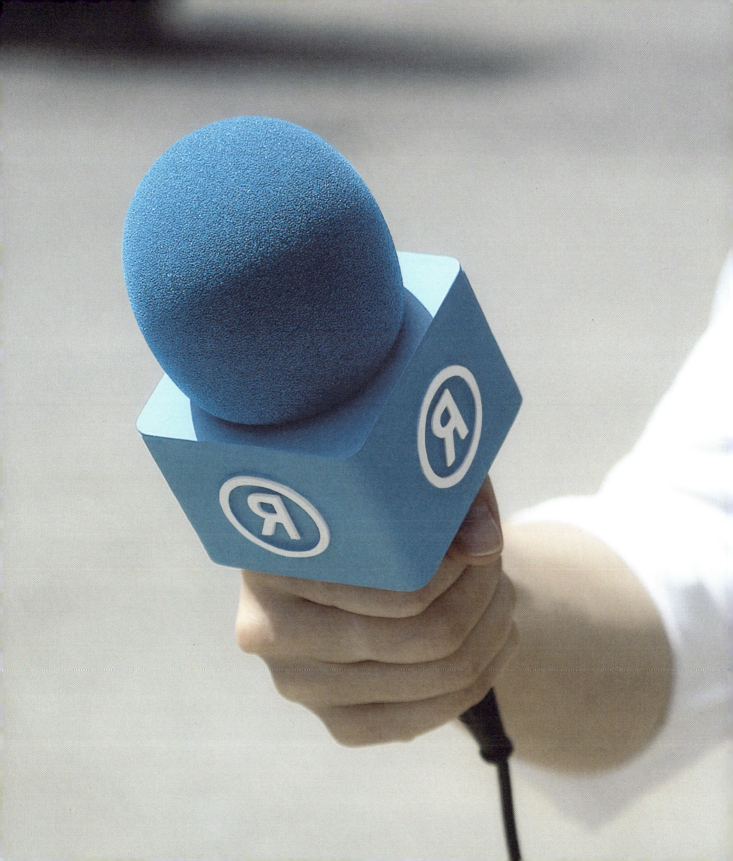

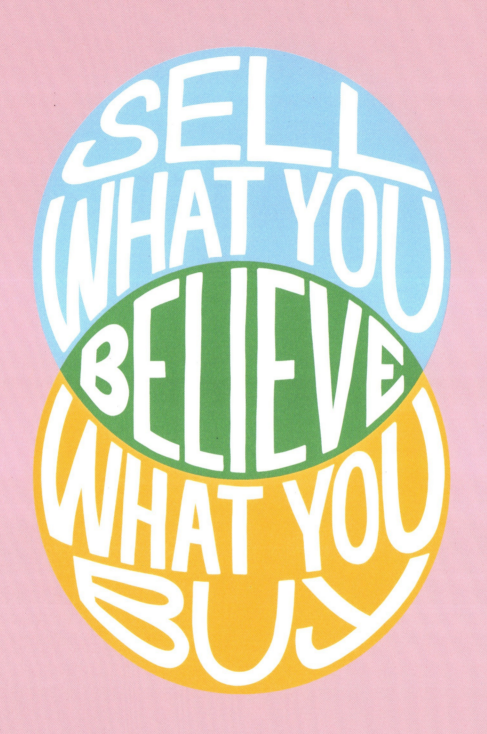

23 The Shared Belief

Want a great strategic insight?
Look for a shared belief.

Before you can create an amazing solution, you need an amazing strategy. That's a given in virtually any creative business.

Many companies isolate strategic thinking in dedicated departments. In the ad business, "account planners" are charged with generating strategic insights, but are often walled-off from the writers, art directors, and designers who will actually solve the creative problem.

At Rethink, we've always believed that strategy is a team sport. Our account planners collaborate closely with their creative and account peers. But the best strategic thinking is more than collaborative. It needs to be grounded in humanity. It needs to be relevant. It needs a Shared Belief.

In our business, many brands have focused almost exclusively on what makes them different—thus the historical obsession with the "unique selling proposition." But in this digital age, when the measure of success is how many people share your communication with friends and family, branded content is seen as a direct reflection of the person sharing it—so talking only about yourself guarantees you'll be ignored. You need to find common ground with your audience if you want them to amplify your message.

Let's use the automotive sector as an example. Nobody just wakes up one day and says, "You know what? I'm a Volvo guy." Very few brands are so strong that people identify with the brand for its own sake. More often than not, it's something shared between the person and the brand that brings them together: "Volvo values passenger safety. I value my family's safety. I value Volvo."

A shared belief can be an ambition, hope, fear, aesthetic… you get the idea. This kind of thinking can be applied to virtually any creative problem in any industry. The Shared Belief is the sweet spot where business and humanity intersect.

24 The Cocktail Party Test

The first job of any idea is to generate chatter.

People hate advertising. All sorts of studies prove it.[13] But over the years, we've noticed a strange thing: if you go to any gathering and wait long enough, someone will almost always bring up an ad, whether it's a campaign they saw or a product they discovered through brilliant marketing. We always tell our clients, "Our job is to get your content talked about. If you pass the Cocktail Party Test, chances are your idea is making a difference."

Ideas that get people talking in real life are probably also causing a stir online. So how do you create an idea that blows up the internet, that becomes the thing everyone's talking and/or tweeting about?

One of the key things our writers and art directors look for during Peer Review (p. 143) is a visceral, emotional reaction to an idea. If an idea is supposed to be funny, did they laugh out loud, or barely crack a smile? If we're going for heartstrings, did we elicit chills or even a tear or two? If not, we know we need to KG (p. 173).

If an idea doesn't provoke a gut reaction it's not going to provoke conversation.

Another way to get a sense of the "stickiness" of your idea is by asking yourself what it would look like as a press headline. What would be the most exciting angle that would be splashed across the front page? Which headline would make you, your mom, and everyone you know click "share"? This tip is no big secret, nor can we take credit for it (see Find It, Steal It & Make It Your Own, p. 89)—the creative minds at Crispin Porter + Bogusky have always been vocal proponents of "What's the headline?" and it shows through in their highly shareable work.

In short: a strong idea should be clear enough to be shared over the phone, in an elevator, as a headline, in a Facebook post, or at a swanky upscale party. It should ring the bell not just for awards judges, but for everyday people and media outlets, too.

Did you see this?

Yeah, Molson Canadian took a beer fridge to Indonesia!

Who would you call first in a time of need?

- Local radio station (0.2%)
- 911 (0.6%)
- Mom (2.2%)
- Traffic (97%)

Where's the first place you go when you have a problem?

To cry in the bathroom

To cry in the stairwell because the bathroom was full

To cry in the bathroom, then talk to Traffic

To talk to Traffic

Avg. amount of bullshit Traffic has protected you from

26.892 Kg

Avg. amount of times Traffic has told you to cc Traffic

2.1317 MM

On a happiness scale, how much better is your life with Traffic?

With Traffic

Without Traffic

0   Happiness %   100

When has Traffic saved your ass?

- When you were drowning (4%)
- When your hair was on fire (13%)
- When you ended up in jail (26%)
- When you forgot how to breathe (55%)

What has Traffic taught you?

- How to be a human being (16%)
- To ask for help before it's too late (22%)
- To embrace the Rethink process (25%)
- It's okay to say no (37%)

25 Traffic

Keep projects (and people) from crashing into each other.

Creative businesses are like airports. Briefs are landing, crews are hustling, and projects big and small are taking flight all over the place. They're bustling, frenetic environments.

But who gets priority on the crowded runway? Which crew climbs aboard which project? And who's up in the control tower making sure all the planes don't collide in mid-air, causing mass chaos and a very expensive mess? At an airport, it's the air traffic controller. At Rethink, we just call it Traffic. Some other creative companies have traffic managers, but very few give those managers the kind of clout Rethink does.

The job of Traffic, whether it's an individual or a team, is to manage creative resources. If the creative department is the engine of your company's machine, then Traffic is the transmission. It distributes power from the engine to wherever it's most needed. When a brief lands, Traffic looks at all the creative teams available, including each team's workload, capacity, and skill set, and decides which is the best fit. This is unlike many companies, where senior leaders are able to walk into a creative department and talk directly to writers, designers, and art directors about assigning a project or booking a meeting.

Traffic doesn't just assign projects—it shepherds them all the way through the Rethink Machine. After every creative check-in, the team goes straight to the Traffic desk and lets them know how much more work is required. If a timeline changes, Traffic is the first to know. And on any email related to creative resourcing, Traffic must be cc'd.

Keeping all the planes in the air requires obsessive levels of communication. A Traffic manager should make a point of checking in with every single creative employee at least once per week, making the rounds and taking detailed notes. It's not enough to simply check timesheets (see Output vs. Hours, p. 183)—Traffic needs to be right on the pulse of the creative department, with an eye on everyone's capacities, stress levels, and even their extracurricular activities.

The benefits of having a powerful Traffic system extend well beyond project management. By ensuring that creatives aren't spread too thin, Traffic provides a psychological safety net. If anyone gets overwhelmed they can go to Traffic and ask for some projects to be diverted. And having a single nexus point for all incoming projects insulates creatives from distracting logistical work, allowing them to calmly focus on the task at hand.

It takes a special type of person to run Traffic. They need to be natural hustlers with great people skills, flexibility, the ability to think on their feet, and a knack for multi-tasking. And they have to do it all day in, day out, while wrangling dozens of creatives. Great Traffic managers are like unicorns, but they're out there. We've found that the most successful Traffic people tend to come from the service or hospitality industries—managers of busy restaurants or hair salons, for example.

There's a myth surrounding creative workplaces: the idea that creativity requires a certain level of chaos to fully thrive. But creativity without discipline can be inefficient and, frankly, exhausting. Despite their reputations, creatives actually appreciate a little structure in their lives—and it can keep a lot more planes up in the air.

26 Office Hours

Instead of playing chase-the-creative-director, keep daily Office Hours.

It's not uncommon for a company to rely on "fly-bys" as the means of providing creative feedback. In many advertising and design shops, creative teams wait for an opportune moment to share work with their creative director; if they can't wrangle a face-to-face meeting, they often wait into the night for feedback via email or voicemail.

This free-flowing approach might seem efficient, but it does more harm than good. It leads to anxious teams pacing in the hallway, waiting their turn to grab a few minutes with their CD, who then gives less thoughtful, more knee-jerk feedback—and gets less of their own work done due to the constant interruptions.

Office Hours are a simple-yet-effective system that we've borrowed from the academic world. Each day, a block of every CD's schedule is dedicated to reviewing creative work. Teams book Office Hours in fifteen- or thirty-minute blocks through Traffic (p. 101), then bring their work to the appointment. Everyone knows when a CD will be available for feedback, and CDs can better plan out their own days and be far more productive.

Having their next OH session on the books helps creative teams keep a project top-of-mind and moving forward—and it prevents them from leaving projects to the last minute. On larger projects it can help to map out all the Office Hours in advance, building in a series of check-ins all the way up to the presentation.

Office Hours might be the single best form of mentorship a company can offer (but see also Founder Facetime, p. 73). Focused one-on-one attention and coaching from leadership is exactly what young creative people crave. It helps them develop their skills faster, gives them insight into the thought process behind the feedback, and gives them a chance to voice their opinions.

Because this experience is so valuable, we try to allow adequate blocks of time. A session should be long enough for the team to share their work, discuss it, and then hear feedback straight from the source (for feedback tips, see DFIU, p. 81). If there are multiple decision-makers in the room, the team can step out for a minute while they align on feedback (also known as "not fighting in front of the kids").

This format is the ideal practice venue for client presentations. Teams should always present their work verbally in OH, just like they would for the client. We always try to do OH in person, with phone calls or video chats as a backup. Explaining an idea out loud as succinctly as possible to someone who hasn't heard it before is the best way to test it for clarity and impact (see The Cocktail Party Test, p. 97).

Yes, there are times when Office Hours can be circumvented. Some things are so urgent that a quick fly-by or email is all you need to keep the project moving. But these should be the exception, not the rule (and even fly-bys should be booked through Traffic). Be vigilant about Office Hours, and you'll ensure that your product gets the focused attention it deserves.

27 Over-Over-communicate

Overcommunication prevents surprises and supports a culture of openness.

In the introduction to this section (p. 84), we introduced the concept of the Rethink Machine, our process for developing ideas. The oil in this Machine is communication. As a project moves through the Machine, overcommunication is built into every step of the process. Without communication to keep it running smoothly, the Machine breaks down—often in spectacular fashion.

Like any corporate value, a commitment to overcommunication starts at the top. If you're an owner or founder, every "What do I want to do?" decision should immediately be followed by "Who do I need to talk to?" When you think about it, running a company is really just an ongoing series of conversations. And that conversation needs to be informed by conversations at every level of the company.

To get everyone on the same page, every project should kick off with an all-hands-on-deck meeting that includes representatives from every department: strategy, accounts, creative, traffic, and production. The Kickoff is a key forum for discussion of the project as a whole. Potential roadblocks are identified, timelines are debated, CDs can weigh in on strategy, producers can flag any budgetary issues that might affect the creative (e.g., the number of talent they can afford), and everyone at the table gets their voice heard. Kickoffs are a great way to reinforce the idea that you are working as one team toward a shared goal.

Throughout the project, check-ins should be booked in advance—not just with the core team but with producers, media partners, suppliers... anyone who needs to be heard. And if at any time anyone feels overwhelmed, the onus is on them to put their hand up or talk to Traffic (p. 101) before the problem escalates.

For bigger projects, you may want to overcommunicate even more by booking a ten-minute stand-up "huddle" to start the day. In addition to aligning on the tasks and objectives for the day, huddles reinforce the feeling of being on a team, working together to overcome problems and achieve a common goal. Huddles are the perfect venue to raise potential issues and deal with them swiftly. (Note: to make sure your huddles don't turn into hour-long meetings, you may want to take the chairs out of the room.)

Overcommunication might feel repetitive, but it's reliable. Think of it as a failsafe. If you were hit by a bus tomorrow, would your company and your team have all the information they need to keep going? This is the approach taken by NASA—they build verbal and technical redundancies into their systems intentionally, to ensure that no matter what happens, critical knowledge is retained.[14] Overcommunication isn't an inefficiency, but a strength.

WORK IN PAIRS 	**BE THE BALL** 	**CHANGE THE TOOLS** 
MAKE LISTS LISTS LISTS LISTS LISTS LISTS LISTS LISTS LISTS LISTS	**IMAGINE HOW SOMEONE ELSE WOULD SOLVE THE PROBLEM** 	**TAKE A WALK** 
CHANGE THE MEDIUM 	$1+1=3$	**START AT THE END** 

28 How to Have an Idea

A pair of simple tools to get you started.

There are many books and websites full of useful tips for generating ideas. This book is not one of those, but we felt like we'd be remiss if we didn't include at least a couple of our go-to idea-generating tools. So here are two that we've gone back to time and time again. They're incredibly simple, incredibly effective, and were involved in much of the work we're most proud of.

The first is 1 + 1 = 3. You're familiar with the idea that the whole is stronger than the sum of its parts, but this works especially well when you combine two seemingly unrelated things. Don't be afraid to smash together words, images, concepts, or objects and see what you get. We often use other tools in this section, like Fast & Loose (p. 133) or the 1-or-100 Rule (p. 139), to look at lots of unrelated things in the hopes of finding a winning pair. Fridge plus passport equals passport-operated beer fridge. WestJet plus Vegas equals giant roulette wheel on desert floor you can play from a plane. And so on.

The second tool is called Be the Ball. It's perhaps the simplest path to creative clarity, and is particularly useful in design projects. It's the key to unlocking those "Wow, it's so obvious, how did I not think of that?" ideas. To Be the Ball, you adopt the subject or theme of your project as its visual language. For a butcher client, we made business cards that look like salami and hang in string netting like cured meats. To stop people from driving drunk, we made drink coasters out of sheet metal from car wrecks. You get the idea.

Throughout this book you'll see a bunch of examples of the power of these two simple formulas—definitive proof that sometimes the best insights are the simplest ones.

1 + 1 = 3

① **RETHINK EXPLODING HEAD**

When we launched Rethink, we wanted to make a bold statement. This logo was intended to show what we planned to do, without resorting to clichés.

② **THE WALRUS TALKS**

The Walrus magazine hosts a series of thought-provoking speakers across the country. Our logo for the events represents both spirited dialogue and the spirit of a certain large sea mammal.

1 + 1 = 3

① **KOZMIC SOUND**

The "Koz" was sound-house owner Wayne Kozak. We combined two universal icons, representing audio speakers and UFOs, to stand out in a crowded field.

② **WILDFLOWER**

Wildflower is a cannabis brand that emphasizes wellness. This simple logo combines a leaf with the universal symbol for pharmacy and medical needs.

③ **KING PONG**

Rethinkers love Ping-Pong. To mark our annual staff tournament, we create a new logo each year. This one requires very little explanation.

1 + 1 = 3

① **ROWAN'S LAW**

This Government of Ontario initiative combined a stop sign with a human brain to warn of the long-term effects of sports concussions on young minds.

② **HUDSON ELECTRIC**

The beauty of some ideas is the sheer number of ways you can complete the 1 + 1 equation, as in this identity for a team of electrical contractors.

③ **KING KOIN**

What do you get when you throw a crown, some coins, and a T-shirt into the spin cycle? Something like this bold identity for a Vancouver laundromat.

②

③

1+1=3

① RICKARDS ST. PATRICK'S DAY

Rickards is Canada's original craft brewer. To help stand out in bars during Saint Patrick's Day, we created this simple logo for all manner of Paddy's Day merch.

② CANADIAN PRESS

It took several on-the-street Peer Review sessions to get this logo just right. The quotes needed to be placed at exactly the right height to get 100 percent comprehension.

③ T-SHIRT PRINTING

A business with a name like T-Shirt Printing deserves an equally direct and simple logo. We created various logos riffing off classic T-shirt designs.

④ BUMPER TO BUMPER

This chain of auto parts retailers truly offers an amazing selection—thus the name. We created two stylized bumpers to form a B that also brackets their product range.

③

④

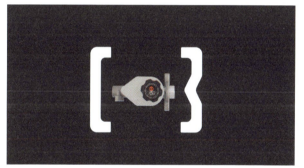

1 + 1 = 3

① **PLAYLAND MEGAPHONE**

Another example of a visually driven 1 + 1 concept for Playland. This campaign also featured silhouettes that combined teens with an air horn and a garden hose.

② **PLAYLAND COASTER TOILET**

Sometimes you can deliver your entire message without a single word of copy, as in this poster promoting Playland's iconic wooden coaster.

③ **PLAYLAND STUFFIES**

Teens love vomit jokes; our clients, not so much. This series of stuffies direct from Playland's arcades managed to make the point in a non-offensive way.

1 + 1 = 3

① **THERMAL DISCOUNT**

We placed this kiosk atop Montreal subway stairs. A special camera would gauge exertion levels and print out Sports Experts deals that rose with body temperature.

② **UBER SAFE**

Take one ride-sharing app, add a working breathalyzer apparatus, and you get an innovative way to promote a safe ride home. We created these kiosks and placed them in busy bar districts. People would blow into the breathalyzer with a straw. If they were over the limit, the kiosk automatically hailed a free Uber ride. The kiosk debuted in Toronto but soon made appearances in cities as far away as Brazil.

③ **CANADIAN FAIR TRADE LONG TAGS**

We combined real stories of abused sweatshop workers with clothing tags to create powerful indictments of the fast-fashion industry.

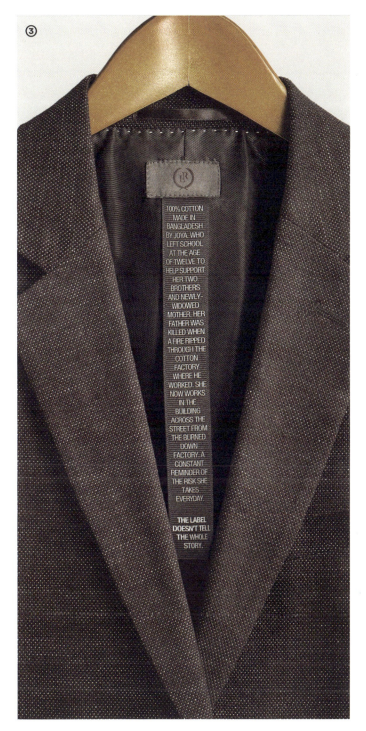

③ 100% COTTON. MADE IN BANGLADESH BY JOYA, WHO LEFT SCHOOL AT THE AGE OF TWELVE TO HELP SUPPORT HER TWO BROTHERS AND NEWLY-WIDOWED MOTHER. HER FATHER WAS KILLED WHEN A FIRE RIPPED THROUGH THE COTTON FACTORY WHERE HE WORKED. SHE NOW WORKS IN THE BUILDING ACROSS THE STREET FROM THE BURNED DOWN FACTORY. A CONSTANT REMINDER OF THE RISK SHE TAKES EVERYDAY.

THE LABEL DOESN'T TELL THE WHOLE STORY.

100% COTTON. MADE IN SIERRA LEONE BY TEJAN. THE FIRST FEW TIMES HE COUGHED UP BLOOD HE HID IT FROM HIS FAMILY. THEY COULDN'T AFFORD MEDICAL TREATMENT AND HE COULDN'T RISK LOSING HIS LONG-TIME JOB AT THE COTTON PLANTATION. WHEN HE FELL INTO A SEIZURE ONE DAY IT COULD NO LONGER BE IGNORED. THE DIAGNOSIS WAS PESTICIDE POISONING. THE LACK OF PROPER PROTECTIVE CLOTHING HAS LEFT HIM WITH LEUKEMIA AT THE AGE OF 34. HE HAS TWO DAUGHTERS. ONE OF THEM STARTS WORK AT THE FACTORY NEXT YEAR.

THE LABEL DOESN'T TELL THE WHOLE STORY.

100% COTTON. MADE IN CAMBODIA BY BEINLY, NINE YEARS OLD. HE GETS UP AT 5 AM EVERY MORNING TO MAKE HIS WAY TO THE GARMENT FACTORY WHERE HE WORKS. IT WILL BE DARK WHEN HE ARRIVES AND DARK WHEN HE LEAVES. HE DRESSES LIGHTLY BECAUSE THE TEMPERATURE OF THE ROOM HE WORKS IN REACHES 35 DEGREES. THE DUST IN THE ROOM FILLS HIS NOSE AND MOUTH. HE WILL MAKE LESS THAN A DOLLAR, FOR A DAY SPENT SLOWLY SUFFOCATING. A MASK WOULD COST THE COMPANY TEN CENTS.

THE LABEL DOESN'T TELL THE WHOLE STORY

Be the Ball

① **COLOURIST CARD**

Alissa is a film colourist. Colour is her craft, essentially. The cards are blind embossed on an iridescent paper that reflects light in a crazy bouquet of wonder.

② **SANDPAPER CARD**

Nothing could be simpler than this card made from sandpaper, with typography to match— proof that an economic solution can also be innovative.

③ **RETHINK CARDS**

We commissioned a die-cut punch machine so that every Rethinker could reuse their unwanted business cards and promote us at the same time.

④ **BIKE TOOL CARD**

This card for a bike repair shop was made from stiff aluminum with die-cut holes that created handy tools for tightening screws and spokes out on the open road.

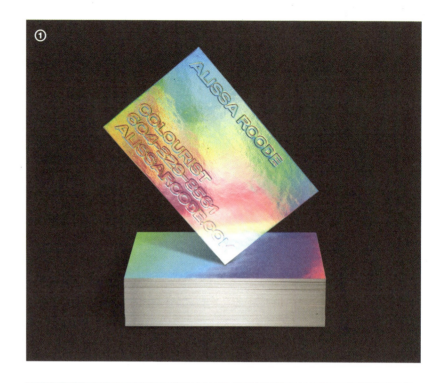

③

④

Be the Ball

① **CREDIT COUNSELLING CARD**

Sometimes half a card tells the whole story, as in this case where we printed business cards to look like destroyed credit cards, complete with real plastic and chips.

② **FILM EDITOR CARD**

The mechanics of film editing are simple: chop up footage and rearrange it. So that's exactly what we did with Megan O'Connor's info.

③ **BLIM CARDS**

To help promote this community art centre's screen-printing program, we created a series of screened cards with functioning mesh, each featuring a different artist.

④ **EDIBLE SURVIVOR CARD**

Who says dark humour and business cards can't mix? This business offers survival gear for adventurers—and a free sample of pressed beef jerky to prove the point.

③

④

Be the Ball

① PASS THE BILL

Leaf Forward, a cannabis business accelerator, celebrated the passing of Bill C-45 (legalizing cannabis) by printing all 152 pages in edible ink on rolling papers.

② SCROLLING MARATHON

Sports Experts wanted to celebrate the perseverance of Montreal marathoners with this demonstration that rewarded users who scrolled the site's 42.2 km length.

③ DESIGNTHINKERS IDENTITY

Design concepts based on eyeballs have been used for years. We knew we'd need to find a fresh way in for this identity system for a series of Canadian design conferences. So we created thousands of versions of eyes, each with a different "pupil." These included dozens of executions in the conference program and printed materials, plus custom eyes for every conference participant, and an app where attendees could create and share their own eyeball GIFs.

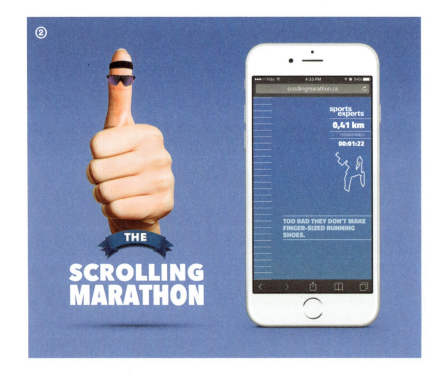

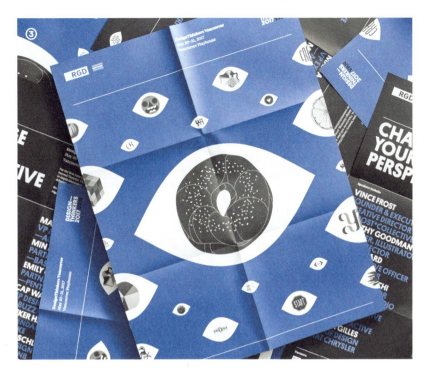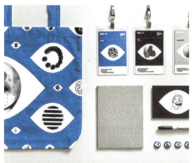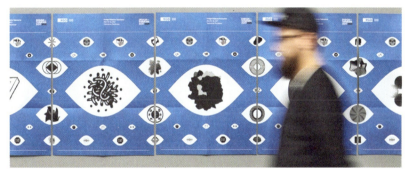

Be the Ball

① **A&W LAST STRAWS**

A&W was the first fast-food restaurant in North America to stop using plastic straws. With the leftovers, we created this art installation to celebrate change for the better.

② **SHAW INTERNET CAFÉ**

Shaw, Western Canada's largest internet provider, prove they understand internet culture with a café full of delicious emoji and meme-themed baked goods.

③ **ORKIN STICKY POSTER**

This poster for Orkin pest control services was blank at first—until bugs got caught in the clear adhesive we sprayed in the shape of the logo. Time told the story.

④ **CRASH COASTERS**

What better way to stop drunk drivers than reaching them while still in the bar? We made these powerful coasters out of metal from actual car wrecks.

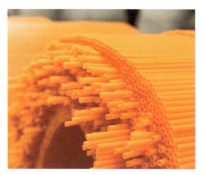

29 Fast & Loose

When generating ideas, don't worry about refining them, just get them down on the page.

We helped Molson take hockey to new heights with an ice rink on top of a skyscraper.
←

When you have a new idea, it can be extremely tempting to jump ahead and imagine the final form. It's understandable, really—everyone wants to see their ideas brought to life. They see a spark of potential and want to pour gas on the fire.

Advanced computer programs have made it almost too easy to take the germ of an idea and present it as a finished concept, but we still believe in the power of old-school pen and paper. We have a rule here for designers and art directors who love to skip ahead to execution: no machines allowed at the concept stage. Writing it down requires zero computer skills, and according to some studies can even make you smarter.[15]

No matter what you're creating, instead of running to the computer to open Photoshop it's best to resist the urge to go deep—just get the idea down in its simplest form, and then Keep Going (p. 173). The same principle applies to any creative problem. Instead of writing a script, write ten short blurbs about different angles the script could take. Instead of crafting a logo in Illustrator, fill a notebook with sketches.

And above all, don't censor yourself. Write down as many ideas as you can in five minutes. Let your hand move freely across the page. Transcribe your stream of consciousness, "er"s and "uh"s and all. Never discard a thought because it feels odd—get it on paper and put it on the wall. You can always take it down later.

No amount of executional polish can save a weak concept. Every minute you spend going deep on your first idea is a minute that could have been spent coming up with more, better ideas. And a great idea will still be great whether it's scribbled on a Post-it or doodled in a sketchbook.

When you train your staff to stay fast and loose at this stage, you give them permission to venture into creative territories they would otherwise never explore. You free their minds to engage with weirder, newer, fresher ideas. You teach them the value of not being too precious. And you save them countless hours wasted moving pixels around on a screen.

Fast & Loose

  **WESTJET
DESERT ROULETTE**

Such a simple idea, such a challenge to execute. Flyers to Vegas played this giant wheel from the sky to win prizes—and the installation broke two world records for its sheer size and luminosity.

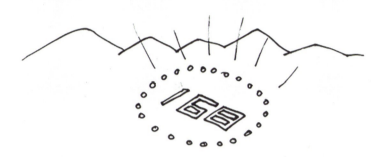

Fast & Loose

① **COAST CAPITAL FREE VENDING MACHINE**

The fun here was finding free stuff to give to passersby. We stocked the unit with everything from used hairbrushes to broken dolls, and still "sold out"!

② **SCIENCE WORLD GOLD BILLBOARD**

The original sketch of this billboard (covered in real gold) didn't include the key media-enticing addition of a security guard to watch over the sign twenty-four hours a day.

③ **CAREX MINI STORAGE**

Keeping the concept simple allows more time for exploration of final visual style after the ad is approved. We considered dozens of illustrators before striking gold.

Fast & Loose

① BC LIONS BOOKENDS

The original sketch was simple as could be. What elevated the final execution was an obsessive attention to craft, including creating custom ceramic figurines.

② BC LIONS SCARED FAN

"Fast & Loose" can even convey complex human emotions and personality types. This series showed fans from competing teams reacting to yet another Lions trouncing.

30 The 1-or-100 Rule

Your best idea could be your first or your hundredth—but you can't know for sure until you've come up with a hundred.

Solving creative problems isn't some ethereal, mystical process, and you don't have to be a genius to do it. The key is trial and error. Anyone who's ever worked at Rethink will tell you that we get to quality through quantity.

The 1-or-100 Rule forces teams to think beyond the obvious. Whatever problem we're trying to solve, we cover entire walls with Post-its and fill notebooks cover to cover. We've found that the most original thinking emerges just when you think you've exhausted your options.

It's important to be rigorous about this early in the process, right after the initial briefing. This is the critical gestation period, when ideas flow freely and easily (see Fast & Loose, p. 133). Capture every last idea, even if you think they're wrong. This phase is when you move past obvious first thoughts and tired ideas into more fertile creative territory. Chances are, if you think of it in the first twenty minutes, someone else has thought of it before. Only once you've peered into every single nook and cranny will you be certain that you've picked the best path forward.

Even then, the work is still just beginning. Goals often change, and generating lots of ideas early on sets you up for success when the problem evolves: you'll have a reservoir of rough thinking you can draw on to adapt your approach. You'll know the problem inside out, so you can solve it even if the goalposts move.

Every creative problem is unique and deserves its own custom solution. And custom solutions require a robust, rigorous exploration. Once you've got at least 100 ideas, it should be clear which ones rise to the top. But if it isn't, there's always the next chapter in this book…

We put the 1-or-100 Rule to the test while generating cover concepts for this book.
→

31 Peer Review

Judging your own work is hard. Trust your peers to give you the unvarnished truth.

Creativity is subjective, which is scary to know going into a client presentation. There are many variables at play, many ways to misinterpret things. Before we share creative work with clients, we arm ourselves with validation from our peers that the work we're sharing is, in fact, great. Peer Review is a system of informal surveys, polls, or in-person meetings with co-workers who represent your target audience. Every company employs a range of people, just like the public at large, which can test drive ideas before you share them with clients. It's not science, but it's a great way to flag issues when the stakes are still low.

    Here's how it works: you choose a group of colleagues, show them a sample of your favourite ideas in rough form, and ask for feedback. We usually seek out three types of respondents—people who think like the target, people who think like awards judges, and people who think like your mom (in other words, a non-jaded real person). Sometimes we tack scribbles to portable corkboards and take them around the office; sometimes we create a simple online poll that we send to Rethinkers across the country. (And many times we've left the office to ask strangers on the street.) The questions we ask vary from project to project, but some of our favourites are:

- "Which of these three scripts do you like the best?"
- "Which one is the clearest?"
- "Which one is the funniest?"
- "Does this headline make sense?"
- "Which one would you click on?"
- "What does this logo look like to you?"

Keep a running tally of the answers, and if possible, record who said what. It often helps to know whether a certain bit of feedback came from an account person or someone in the creative department. Once you have your numbers tallied, it's time to interpret the results. It's important to note that no one person's opinion can kill an idea. Just like with our Culture Check results (see Cheap & Cheerful, p. 187), our rule of thumb is: if one person says something you can ignore them, if two people say it you should listen, and if three people say it you should act. If an idea is the favourite by a landslide, make it your recommendation and consider presenting it first. If an idea gets no votes, kill it. And if nothing is really resonating... KG (p. 173).

You can learn all kinds of useful things from even a quick round of Peer Review. It can tell you if your idea is funny, if it's gross, if it's insensitive or tone-deaf, and most importantly, whether or not it meets the requirements of CRAFTS (p. 149)—is your idea Clear, Relevant, Achievable, Fresh, True, and Shareable?

Going into a presentation with Peer Review results in your back pocket will make you feel confident and prepared to speak to your favourites. It will also put the client at ease to know that you've done your due diligence, which will help them resist the urge to resort to a focus group. Sometimes they're a necessary evil, but generally focus groups are where great creative ideas go to die—good thing your idea has already passed Peer Review! Think of Peer Review as a faster, cheaper, far less painful form of research, that you get to control.

Peer Review is our best defence against unexpected feedback, and our great equalizer when opinions differ. Over the years it has won us many more battles than arguing in boardrooms. When a client trusts the process, they trust us.

Peer Review not only strengthens your product, it helps develop your people, too. It teaches humility and openness to change. It introduces stubborn creative types to the possibility that maybe they're wrong, and discourages them from being precious with their ideas. It makes everyone who participates feel like they contributed to a project or helped make an idea bulletproof. And the more Peer Review your teams do, the more they'll develop that elusive ability to know an amazing idea as soon as they see it.

32 The Ping-Pong Ball Theory

People can only digest one message at a time. Don't overwhelm your audience.

The Ping-Pong Ball Theory is one of our oldest and simplest tools, but it's still as relevant today as it was twenty years ago.

If I throw you one Ping-Pong ball, you'll catch it. But if I throw you five at once, you probably won't catch any. The same goes for communication. If you tell me one message, I'll hear it. But if you hit me with multiple messages, the whole spiel will likely go in one ear and out the other.

It sounds easy enough, but advertisers have been bombarding their audiences with too many Ping-Pong balls since the *Mad Men* era. When we write a creative brief, we ask our clients, "In one simple sentence, what do you want to say?" Too often, the sentence they come up with reads more like a laundry list: "My product is the safest and the simplest and will give you peace of mind and there's a sale on right now!"

There is a solution for this phenomenon: Get your Ping-Pong balls in a row. Commit to saying one thing at a time, then send out multiple pieces of content to your audience, in order, one at a time.

Thanks to digital sequencing algorithms, it's now easier than ever to break your messaging up into bite-sized, easy-to-digest pieces. People who "catch" a Ping-Pong ball (by clicking or spending time on your content) then receive the next ball in the sequence. First you might throw someone a high-level emotional brand message. If they catch that one, maybe throw them a unique feature or benefit. If they catch that one, they're clearly interested and you can throw them an offer.

You'll find this works in any creative business—think about your key messages, prioritize them, and deliver them in a powerful, consistent sequence. In a world that's busier and noisier than ever, simplicity and clarity are the keys to breaking through the clutter. Attention spans continue to shrink, videos get shorter and shorter. You only have time to say one thing before your viewer moves on. But if you hit that one Ping-Pong ball just so—with the right amount of creative spin on it—you can still get your message across.

33 CRAFTS

How to judge a creative idea? Use this simple checklist.

The worst feedback you can get for an idea is, "I just don't like it." Or, "It's not really doing it for me." Vague or subjective feedback is incredibly frustrating because it's impossible to learn from. And if feedback is inconsistent, teams don't know what to shoot for because they feel like the goalposts are moving. Having one consistent, master checklist for ideas makes the whole process feel less subjective and more productive.

When we give internal feedback, whenever possible, we try to bring it back to CRAFTS. It's a great way to get speedy feedback on ideas before showing them to clients.

- Is the idea **Clear**?
- Is it **Relevant** to the target audience?
- Is it **Achievable**, on time and on budget?
- Is it **Fresh** and unique?
- Is it **True** to the brand, and can you back it up?
- Is it **Shareable** on social media?

When teams know the exact criteria by which they'll be judged, they become better at self-editing. They can be precise in their feedback: "I like how clear the idea is, but I feel like I've seen something like it before."

It should be noted that without the "C" in CRAFTS, nothing else really matters. It doesn't matter how relevant or fresh an idea is if it lacks clarity. We're in the communication business after all, not the making-cool-things-for-fun business. Try as you might, you just can't float on RAFTS.

Ideas that make it through the gauntlet are shared with clients. It's important that they know about CRAFTS too, so they know we're not just relying on gut instinct. They take comfort in learning about the science behind our art. And with enough friendly reminders about CRAFTS, our clients eventually learn to judge ideas by the same standards we do.

☑ **CLEAR**
Is your idea simple and understandable?

☑ **RELEVANT**
Will your audience relate to it?

☑ **ACHIEVABLE**
Can it be produced on time and on budget?

☑ **FRESH**
Is it unique and original?

☑ **TRUE**
Is it based on facts, data, and can you back it up?

☑ **SHAREABLE**
Would people want to tell their friends about this?

34 ACTS, not Ads

Let your ideas live in the real world.

As people spend less and less time watching broadcast TV, the reign of the thirty-second commercial is coming to an end (thankfully). The big question in the communications business is: What will replace the old model? How do you reach people who are dispersed across endless streaming platforms and social media sites? One refreshing possibility: the real world.

After our world-famous beer fridge campaign (more on that below), ACTS was coined by Molson CMO Peter Nowland to describe the type of experiential marketing that can lead to global buzz:

- **Authentic**
- **Credible**
- **Tangible**
- **Shareable**

We learned the value of ACTS early in our Rethink years. Our client sold a 3M film that when applied to windows makes them virtually bulletproof (and burglar-proof). We decided to create a real-life demonstration. We took a backlit sign from a transit shelter, removed the bulbs, and covered both glass panels with the film. In between the clear panels, we placed prop money that looked like half a million dollars in U.S. bills.

Then we put it back on the street and watched. Lots of people tried to break the glass—to no avail. We shot some photos of these attempted break-ins, sent them to media contacts, and invited them to come down and give it their best shot. We ended up with over a million dollars in earned media coverage, an amazing result in a pre–viral-media era.

In the years since, we've created dozens of experiences for our clients—and broadened our thinking to include design. We once covered the exterior of Vancouver's Contemporary Art Gallery with thousands of lapel buttons, each expressing a different aspect of contemporary art—e.g., confused, motivated, outraged. We then invited people to take and wear the buttons, thus becoming mobile brand ambassadors for the gallery.

Many of our experiences involve new technologies we develop in tandem with high-tech partners, often sparked during R+D Days (p. 215). For Molson, we arrived at the insight that Canadians are most proud of their country when they're travelling abroad, maple leaf emblazoned on their backpacks. So we created a red beer fridge that could only be opened by inserting a Canadian passport, and stuck it in the middle of London and other points around Europe. Scan your passport, and get a fridge full of Molson Canadian for you and your new friends.

We recorded the beer fridge's journey using 100 percent real people over a period of several days. This video then became the "ad" for Molson. It was first shared with media outlets, thereby ensuring most beer drinkers had seen the footage before any paid media ran. When we sent the fridge to the Sochi Winter Olympics, we sparked a global media gold rush.

These campaigns reinforced for us the power of using experiences to engage people and, crucially, the media. The shareable part is key in the new smartphone world. People can skip ads with the flick of a thumb, so our goal with ACTS is to create thumb-stopping content so good it begs to be shared. This thinking can be applied to any business. In a social media world, experience is king.

ACTS, not Ads

① **3M SECURITY GLASS**

It's quite frankly a miracle that the glass didn't break after dozens of attempts—a testament to 3M's product, and hours of pre-tests with Rethinkers.

② **PILSNER ICE SHACK**

Old Style Pilsner is a favourite in Eastern Canada, whether it's summer or winter. So we created a working bar on a frozen lake, complete with an in-water beer cooler.

③ **MOLSON CANADIAN BEER FRIDGE**

We worked with talented tech partners to help bring the various iterations of the Molson Canadian Beer Fridge to life. Google helped us create a version that required passersby to say the words "I am Canadian" in at least six different languages, which often meant gathering others to help, in order to open the fridge. Over two hundred languages were programmed, including several Indigenous dialects. To celebrate the brand's long history with hockey, we also created a specially reinforced fridge that would only open via a slap shot.

ACTS, not Ads

① **IKEA CLIMATE CHANGE EFFECT**

Small changes to climate can have a big impact. We secretly hiked the temperature in a Toronto IKEA by four degrees, getting attention from shoppers and the media.

② **CAG BUTTON WALL**

Vancouver's Contemporary Art Gallery itself became an art installation, allowing you to wear your feelings about art on your sleeve—or backpack.

ACTS, not Ads

① **FONDATION ÉMERGENCE BRUTAL TRUTHS**

For the 2019 International Day Against Homophobia and Transphobia in Montreal, we took posts from the internet and put them on posters. The police responded in twenty minutes; the hate posts remain online to this day.

② **NO TANKERS VR**

No Tankers has been trying to keep oil tankers out of BC's coastal waters for years. We modified a tourist staple to create a VR overlay of the devastation of a spill in Vancouver's harbours.

35 Shallow Holes

Avoid pitfalls by sharing a broader range of exploration earlier in the process.

It's human nature to fight new ideas that are presented to you, especially the further along they are.[16] That can be a crippling barrier in an idea-based industry like advertising—or technology, or engineering, or architecture, or accounting. When trying to sell an idea, you need a way to overcome the buyer's hard-wired reluctance and get them excited. In our experience, Shallow Holes is that way.

The metaphor works like this: Imagine you're looking for gold on a beach. You could pick out one arbitrary spot and say, "We need to dig exactly there, and nowhere else," and then get started digging a hole to China. Or, you could test different areas: dig a little bit here, a little bit there, and sift through the sand looking for any traces of gold. Which sounds likely to succeed?

Don't waste your time and energy digging deep until you've uncovered a shiny nugget or two. In advertising terms, this means doing a wide initial exploration, testing out various insights against simple executions such as a billboard, a tagline, or a script. For an artist it could mean doing many pencil sketches before putting paint to canvas. You're looking for proof-of-concept at this shallow stage—just enough validation to know it could be worth it to dig deep.

On any given project, you and your team might dig dozens of initial Shallow Holes. You can then narrow them down in Office Hours (p. 105) and put your favourites through Peer Review (p. 143) to find the top candidates to share with the client.

Next comes the key part of Shallow Holes: letting the client see them early, in rough form, so they know you aren't pitching one big idea in a very polished form. This makes clients instantly relax—lack of choice is every client's secret nightmare.

Instead of being force-fed a polished idea, they get to participate in choosing which Shallow Hole (or two) to dig deeper. The key decision-makers now feel like they're in the trenches with you, contributing to the creative process. And because they've provided direction early on, they'll be less likely to reject ideas during the Deep Dive (p. 165). Once you're in the same hole, you're all in it together.

When you do Shallow Holes, you come away knowing there are multiple viable options, and that whichever area the client chooses can be crafted into something great. They'll be excited to see broad exploration and will know they got their money's worth. Even if you haven't quite nailed it yet, the transparency of the process will leave the client feeling confident that if you just keep digging, you'll get there.

36 The Deep Dive

Take your most promising Shallow Holes and dig them deeper.

The Shallow Holes process (p. 161) is like digging six inches deep in a sandbox. Once you've found one or two promising areas, it's time to drill down three hundred feet.

Ideally there's an obvious Shallow Holes winner, but sometimes a client needs to see a couple of deep explorations. In either case, it's important to have a clear list of deliverables. The initial exploration may have included only a brand mantra, a video script, a billboard, and a social post, all in rough form. The Deep Dive (which is really more of a Deep Dig) takes that basic thinking and applies it everywhere the brand connects with people. This means both traditional and new media, but it also extends far beyond advertising—like experiential "stunts," store design, uniforms, customer experience, internal communications, staff development tools, even product ideas.

Part of this process is developing the design "glue" that will hold all of these things together. We often pair designers with art directors and writers to explore a wide range of visual expressions, using Peer Review to come up with a comprehensive design system that includes colour, font, visual style, and tone.

At this point, we usually widen the number of people involved on the client side beyond the core marketing team: We talk to the folks running the call centres and the stores. We find out what tools HR needs to attract and train talent. We brainstorm products and promotional ideas with the appropriate client teams. Some of the eventual ideas will be executed by a client's internal creative team, and we find we get far better buy-in if we involve them early in the process.

Using this process means there's no giant dog-and-pony show to unveil a new brand platform to the top executive. By the time we get to the Deep Dive, everyone has bought into the vision because they've helped shape it right from the start. The final result is a fully realized brand plan that energizes every part of a client's organization.

37 Dealing with Client Input

Give them what they asked for, then show them what they need.

Feedback is inevitable. No matter how brilliant an idea might be, there will virtually always be notes. Providing feedback is the client's job, after all. How you deal with this feedback makes all the difference.

We repeat this simple phrase like a mantra: "Give them what they asked for, then show them what they need." It sums up our philosophy on client input, and is the key to helping great concepts actually get produced.

Our first ironclad rule is to never present a big idea to the client that we wouldn't be happy to produce. If you give the client a safe, boring idea, you shouldn't be surprised if they buy it, and you'd better be ready to deliver. When it comes to more fine-grained feedback, we almost never try to battle each point they raise—that just makes you seem defensive and overly attached to your ideas.

The right response to almost every piece of client feedback is, "That's interesting. We'll look at that." This shows the client you're open to their ideas, and it buys you time to see how your idea would be affected by their suggestions—which in fact often have some merit.

You can use Peer Review (p. 143) to test their changes and come up with something better, then cite your internal feedback to convince them your alternative is clearer, or more original, or more achievable: "We looked at your idea, but then found out it had been done by a competitor. But we took the essence of your thinking to come up with this totally original new idea." (Nothing causes a client to reconsider faster than saying their suggestion has been done by a competitor, or that it will cause the project to go way over budget.)

All of this is simply good client relations. Even if you vehemently disagree with the feedback, making the effort to do the revisions shows that you're open and collaborative, and willing to go above and beyond. In the vast majority of cases, the client appreciates that we did what they asked, but agrees with the new, improved direction.

And if they don't, there's always the next chapter…

What they asked for.

What they need.

38 If It's Wounded, Kill It

When nothing else works, there's always the nuclear option.

Giving the client what they asked for and then showing them what they need (see previous chapter) almost always sells your recommended idea. But sometimes it becomes clear the client's feedback will completely destroy your concept—no matter how much you experiment, tweak, and consult with your peers.

Maybe the client wants you to combine two ideas that won't fit together (the dreaded Frankenstein's monster). Maybe they want to shoehorn too many messages into a single execution. Or maybe it's death by a thousand cuts—so many little changes that the original vision becomes unrecognizable.

If client feedback compromises the underlying concept beyond repair, it's important to acknowledge that and put your poor concept out of its misery. In other words: If It's Wounded, Kill It. (Thanks to the late Mike Hughes of the Martin Agency, who shared this phrase with us at an *Adweek* Creative Seminar.)

The nuclear option should be used rarely, to help preserve its impact. Having the guts to kill an idea in front of a client is powerful—it says in no uncertain terms that we'd rather start over from scratch than produce something that won't work. We have another saying for these situations: The client can kill a great ad, but they need to buy a great ad.

No matter how attached you are to an idea, it's only an idea. And ideas can always be topped. Our advice to creative teams: Go home and have a good cry (and a large glass of wine). Then get back on your bike tomorrow and keep going.

39 KG

The art of achieving quality through quantity: keep going.

Creativity is a numbers game. The more ideas you come up with, the better the end result will be. That's the philosophy that drives our 1-or-100 Rule (p. 139) and the reason we keep the expression of ideas Fast & Loose (p. 133). We believe you can keep improving and evolving ideas until the day before you present them. All you need to do is Keep Going.

At Rethink, we've adopted Keep Going, or KG, as a mini-mantra that speaks to the relentless pursuit of a great creative product. "Keep Going" speaks to the opportunity you'll miss if you settle for "good enough." Could the script be funnier? KG. Could the design be simpler? KG. In our experience, the ability to embrace KGing is what separates great creatives from the merely good. It has been the single biggest driver of Rethink's success.

KGs can happen at any step of the process. First you have to KG until you've done a full 1-or-100. Then you might have to KG on a few half-baked ideas to see if there's anything there.

Peer Review (p. 143) might identify even more things for you to KG on before the presentation. And once you get an idea approved and green lit by the client, you still have to KG the whole way through production all the way to the finish line.

Sometimes when a creative team gets "KG'd" it means they have a problem to solve. It could be something minor, like "How will this TV idea work in social media?" Or it could be something more major, like "What if the hockey rink was on top of a skyscraper?" Really, a creative project is just a series of problems. It's a marathon, not a sprint.

Of course, to KG you need adequate time. Some creative businesses try to arrive at solutions as quickly as possible to help boost their bottom line; others can't KG because they are simply too disorganized, or they don't prioritize rigorous creative exploration. They'll show the client three ideas because that's all they had time to come up with. That's why the Rethink Machine is so important—the more efficient and organized we are, the more time there is to KG.

KG is more than an acronym, it's an attitude. It represents putting in the work, doing the reps, and trusting the process. No shortcuts allowed.

Profit

The trouble with the advertising business is that 90 percent of agencies today are in "profit maximization" mode for their global shareholders. This has led to an unsustainable model where these companies are under constant pressure to deliver profit before anything else. We know it first-hand because we left a great agency eighteen months after it was sold to one of the multinationals.

Our experience at Palmer Jarvis in the '90s was formative. Before the sale, the word "profit" was rarely discussed among senior managers—the focus was squarely on improving our product and pitching new business. After the sale, everything changed. It soon seemed quarterly profit targets were the only topic of conversation.

In the midst of this, we read a book called *Open Minds*, by Andy Law, about an upstart agency in London called St. Luke's. We were inspired by their values-based approach to creating a new kind of agency. They created a co-operative structure, where everyone from the receptionist to the president owned an equal share of the company. This was a little too far-left-leaning for us—but their spirit of innovation was certainly welcome.

St. Luke's taught us the value of looking at the business differently. They'd broken away from a multinational network and created an environment where great people could do great work, freed from typical profit constraints. This helped inspire our priorities: people, product, and profit, in that order.

But don't get us wrong—we're still capitalists (social capitalists, but capitalists nonetheless). Growth is good, especially when it's managed carefully. We've always gone by the adage "If you're growing, you're green." Just to keep up with the cost of inflation, you need to grow by 2 or 3 percent a year. And profit is good, especially as a by-product of great work that is produced efficiently. What's not good is obsessing quarter after quarter about either growth or profit.

We believe in creating the conditions for a healthy profit margin to be delivered each and every year. Our goal is a 15 percent margin, and in great years we've exceeded this.

We believe that we should share our profits with employees and partners. Our plan starts giving at 7.5 percent and grows as our profit grows.

We believe in growing retained earnings to allow us to manage our business independently.

Over the years we've been tested with tough economic conditions and changes in the industry. We've never lost money in any year because we've always been conservative with our P&L and proactive when it comes to managing our costs.

In our worst year, post-2008, we had to cut a third of our work force to break even. Even here, however, we tried to put people first. We were as transparent as possible with our entire staff, and gave everyone leaving twice the government-mandated severance pay. We also vowed to broaden our business base by opening a new office in Toronto, the capital of marketing in Canada. The new office, combined with honest communication with our staff, helped us weather tough times with our culture intact. Pruning the tree helps it prepare for new growth.

Recently, I've been inspired by another book, *Conscious Capitalism*, by Raj Sisodia and John Mackey, a co-founder of Whole Foods. What resonates with me personally—and has been part of our success—is the need to deliver for all stakeholders, not just for shareholders.

Stakeholders before shareholders: such a simple, smart idea. I hope you find some of the other ideas in this section equally inspiring.

Tom Shepansky, Founding Partner

40 Believers Create Believers

Save your soul by only taking on clients you believe in.

Our Head of IT actually got our logo tattooed on his forearm. Believers indeed.

←

At Rethink, our purpose is to create more believers in brands and initiatives we believe in. To achieve that goal, we have to work with the right partners. You'd think this would be a common approach, but it's surprising how few creative businesses really think about who they're doing business with.

We've always said life is too short to work to sell toilet paper. Which is why we avoid formula-driven Consumer Packaged Goods clients. And political government work. And icky things like lotteries or products aimed at kids.

From our first days at Rethink, we kept a whiteboard with three questions we ask ourselves about potential clients: Do we believe in the brand and the people behind it? Do we believe in the potential to do great work? Can they pay our rates?

No matter what, the answer to the first question must be a Yes. This rule keeps us honest and holds us to our values:

people come before product and profit. Plus, life's too short to work with assholes (see No Assholes, p. 21).

If the answers are Yes–Yes–Yes, just tell us where to sign. We're in. Let's schedule the kickoff meeting.

If we get a Yes–No–Yes, we're still in—but we recognize that it will likely be challenging to move the barge off of whatever sandbar it's run aground on (see Barges, Speedboats & Submarines, p. 41). But even though the creative might not be award-winning, at least the people are nice and the added income will allow us to hire more great people of our own. If we go in with tempered expectations, we'll be fine.

If the answers are Yes–Yes–No, we may still be in, but we have a few caveats. We can find creative ways to work on a tighter budget. But if we're going to reduce our rates or do pro bono work (see Change Proposals, p. 221), then the creative potential has to be through the roof. If we believe in the brand or the cause, the people, and our ability to hit consistent home runs, we're in. Otherwise, a polite "no, thank you" is in order.

By sticking to this formula, we attract clients with similar values to ours. We also save a lot of time, money, and energy. When our clients care about the same things we do, that's when the magic happens. Win, win, win.

41 Output vs. Hours

When it comes to fees, output matters much more than watching the clock.

Many creative businesses set an hourly rate, and bill clients for every hour each person spends on the project, often in the form of a "blended" rate. This system misses an important factor: the value of the creative solution. Does this value derive from the quality of the idea, its ability to shift perception and behaviour? Or does it come from a ticking clock? In determining how to charge for our services, we've always believed that it's important to look at the output (creative product) rather than the input (hours spent).

All of our contracts are based on scope—a list of the things we'll actually create for the client. We still have hourly rates for most job functions, which we check against the market at regular intervals, but we're not slaves to our rate card or our timesheets, like many of our competitors. Rather, we simply use our rates, as well as past experience with similar projects, to help estimate a fixed fee for delivering the agreed-upon output.

The advantages of charging for output instead of hours are clear, both for us and for our clients.

For Rethink, a lack of obsession over timesheets means we can have a much leaner accounting department. We've learned that people in the creative business are good at lots of things, but filling out timesheets accurately is not one of them. In some big agencies, several people spend their entire days chasing down missing timesheets and making sure every hour is reconciled. We have an accounting department of seven people for 175 Rethinkers across five offices.

Sometimes we spend more time on a project than we anticipated. If this is because the brief changed or the scope changed, we'll discuss it with our clients. But if the overage is because we spent extra time to find the solution, we never ask for more money. We chalk it up to an investment in our relationship. We can always adjust our fees next time.

Often we deliberately choose to over-invest in a project. This might be to gain valuable experience in a new category. Or to help build a relationship with a big client. Or to support a great cause we believe in. This obviously provides great value for our clients, and is a key part of our retention strategy.

Our clients benefit in other ways, too. If you asked any CMO their biggest complaints about their agency partner, hours that exceeded the original project estimate would probably be near the top of the list. We know first-hand that big clients at multinational agencies get "time dumped" because "they can afford it." Our clients can have confidence that the budget is the budget, and we'll stick to it.

So when you employ a designer, an architect, or anyone in a creative business, think about the value they bring, not how much time they spend on any given task. We bet you'll get better output, and you'll spend less time sweating over whether they spent the "right" amount of time on the solution.

42 Cheap & Cheerful

Invest in people, not furniture.

We love IKEA furniture. Even before they became our client in 2017, we were always big fans. With IKEA desks, chairs, and credenzas dating back to 1999, our office looks a bit like an IKEA Hall of Fame. Their products are simple, modern, and affordable, and it's easy to buy matching products as we grow. And all the money we save goes back to our people.

Of course, we did want to add our own touches of flair to our cheap and cheerful design. We added an assortment of maps, globes, and quirky thrift-store clocks to make the space our own. We made lighting fixtures out of white traffic cones, installed Astroturf (p. 189) instead of carpet, built the Lego room (see Space to Play, p. 29), and put Ping-Pong tables in our boardrooms to help us demonstrate the Ping-Pong Ball Theory (p. 147).

With the money we don't spend on expensive furnishings we can hire more people—and invest in them once they're here.

That can mean small things like free beer and sodas, and big things like conferences, classes, and leadership coaching.

You can have an office that's cool, quirky, and impressive to your clients without breaking the bank. And your people will thank you for it.

43 Astroturf

To keep staff from seeking new pastures, keep yours as green as they can be.

When it comes to office decor, we're big fans of Astroturf. Not because it's cheap and durable (which it is). Not because it looks cool (which it does). And not because of its miraculous ability to trap and retain dog hair (don't get us started on the dog hair). No, we like Astroturf because we like to live our metaphors.

To us, Astroturf is a daily reminder that creative people are always looking for greener pastures. Talented people will always wonder if life is better somewhere else: other shops, other clients, other projects, other careers. So they pack up and leave. If we want to retain the top talent, we have to create the greenest, most lush and fertile pasture in town. We have to be the shop that everyone's talking about:

- "Did you hear about Rethink?"
- "What's it like over there?"
- "I hear they don't have timesheets."

- "I hear they get to work from home."
- "I hear they have free beer."

Luring those people over to our side of the fence feeds into our cycle of continued success: Hire top talent. Produce the best work. Attract new business. Hire top talent. And so on.

We make sure the Astroturf is greener with regular check-ups twice a year. We do a company-wide Culture Check with fewer than twenty key questions. Simple ones like:

- Are you happy at Rethink?
- Do you feel like there's good communication?
- Is there good work-life balance?
- Is this a place where you feel like you can do the best work of your career?

We take the answers very seriously indeed. In fact, many of the tools in this book came directly from the Culture Check. For instance, we introduced Founder Facetime (p. 73) in response to lower scores on mentorship.

And because we're independent, we can invest in little things that make a difference in people's lives, like free beverages, spontaneous celebrations, and days off instead of mandatory overtime. All of these things become unaffordable if you're constantly chasing 25 percent profit margins, as is par for the course at most multinationals.

So ask yourself… what's your Astroturf? And are you keeping it as green as it can possibly be?

44 Promote from Within

Building a winning team with rookies pays off in the long run.

Let's say you're the GM of a sports franchise. There are two very different approaches you can take to build a championship team: You can play the long game, drafting the top young prospects and growing them into stars. Or you can play the short game, making trades to bring in proven top-level talent. The first option requires you to invest in scouting, mentorship, and development. But the second option is costly, too—you'll pay a hefty price for outside players who might not fit into your locker-room culture.

As you can probably guess from the title of this section, we prefer the first option. Since rookies are a lot cheaper than proven stars, it helps control costs—especially in a creative business where senior people are well compensated (much like in many sports). But hiring and promoting rookies pays in other ways, too.

Promoting from within allows you to protect and preserve the culture that you've so carefully created for your company.[17] Instead of bringing years of baggage and pre-existing notions from other agencies, your employees will be steeped in your culture from the start of their careers. Instead of teaching cynical old dogs new tricks, you can focus on house-training malleable, eager-to-please puppies. They will internalize your company's values, philosophies, and priorities, and will pass them on to others.

It is critical to ensure employees at all levels stay motivated. When you promote from within, everyone sees that it is in fact possible to climb the ladder (though the ladder shouldn't have too many rungs—see Flat Structure, p. 199). Senior promotions open up space for intermediate promotions, and so on, all the way down to the interns. This instills a sense of intrinsic motivation in employees—the feeling that they control their own destinies; that success depends not on outside forces like hiring or upper management politics, but on their ability to perform in the role they've been given. Every employee should always believe that they're working toward something and have room to grow.

And an internal promotion signals to your entire staff that you trust them and want them to thrive. While a senior outside-hire can breed resentment and uncertainty among the lower ranks, internal promotions create a sense that everyone's pulling in the same direction, and pulling each other up. And those employees who you promote will move mountains to prove that you put your trust in the right person.

By the time a Rethinker reaches their first promotion, their creative juices are around 85 percent Rethink Kool-Aid. They're more loyal, more emotionally invested in the success of the company, and more likely to stick around longer. Promote from within instead of hiring an overpaid mercenary, and you'll inspire a believer in your brand.

45 Shared Leadership

If you're playing the long game, learn to share the load—and the leadership.

Rethink doesn't have a CEO, and we've never had a president. This was a deliberate choice on day one. We believe having one person in charge of a company—especially a creative company—is a potential landmine. Who is the single person in charge, and what part of the business do they represent? Many advertising and design agencies, despite being in the business of creativity, are actually run by account people who are trained in the business side of the business. This has always struck us as more than a little counterintuitive.

From the beginning, we've structured the company to share leadership among a small group. For us, less is more. A group of two, three, or four is small enough to be nimble, but large enough to represent all sides of the business. In Rethink's case, Tom represented the business side, and Chris and Ian the creative side. For our first decade, it worked remarkably well. Now, twenty years since our founding, we're making sure that this shared model is scalable well into the future.

We started by adding new partners to the mix. In many businesses, becoming a partner is an onerous and protracted experience. Potential partners often have to pay their dues—in both time and money. Some have to mortgage their homes to buy shares in a company. At Rethink, we *gift* equity to our partners. This makes the idea of partnership far more accessible, so more people (and particularly young people) can realistically aspire to one day make it to the top. We had an employee go from intern to partner in only five years—proof that Rethink is a meritocracy, not an autocracy.

We now have close to twenty partners at Rethink, each of whom owns real shares in the company. They come from every office and every part of the company—from the Creative Department, to Strategy, to Account Management, to Production.

From this group, we assign a smaller group of Managing Partners to run their respective offices. The MPs are meant to reflect our founding leadership structure, with a small group of two, three, or four partners in charge. The MPs in each office report to the three founders, who now act as the company's hands-on Board of Directors.

It's a structure that can be handed down to future generations, and replicated across multiple locations. It will also protect Rethink's independence, which is the root of our success.

46 Flat Structure

Strive to have fewer rungs on your corporate ladder.

As companies grow, so do their corporate structures. Job titles get longer and more specific as more layers are added to the hierarchy. The idea behind these structures is to create clearly delineated roles and responsibilities, which is supposed to somehow increase efficiency.

We believe they do the opposite. Layers of hierarchy means layers of approval, which dilute the creative product (death by a thousand cuts, all the way up the ladder). And hyper-specific roles tell people to stay in their lane, which inhibits creativity. By keeping the corporate structure simple, we've removed many relatively meaningless distinctions.

People should be defined by what they create, not their titles. If you're a Rethink copywriter, for example, don't expect to see "junior," "intermediate," or "senior" in your job title. A writer is a writer is a writer.

Small promotions put people in small boxes. With an overly nested system of titles, instead of hearing "We should put Sean on that. He can handle it!" you might hear the dreaded "We can't give that project to a Junior." There's no reason why a star "junior" writer shouldn't get to own a juicy, senior-level project. When more people are on the same level, they're given a larger box to move around in. Besides, there are plenty of other ways to show appreciation beyond promotions (see The Power of Appreciation, p. 33).

We do still have Creative Directors— the ones who get to approve the work—but there's no requirement to put in a given number of years to earn the gig. If they can do the job, they can do the job.

Remember: it's not about years of service, it's about talent and hard work. You want your people making great work, not squabbling over seniority. And you want them to feel like reaching the top is actually achievable, which is a tough sell if they're ten promotions away. When advancement feels realistic, people will work harder and stay with the company longer. And that's good for the bottom line.

In short—the fewer rungs on the ladder, the less intimidating the climb.

47 How to Share Profits

If the company wins, we all win.

First, a disclaimer: profit sharing is a minefield. When done wrong, it can lead to disgruntled staff, unreasonable expectations, and perceived favouritism. But if thoughtfully implemented and fairly distributed, profit sharing helps with recruitment and is a useful tool for rewarding the collective efforts of your staff.

In the traditional agency world, most companies do profit sharing wrong (if they do it at all), only starting the sharing when profit margins hit 18, 20, or even 25 percent. And even then, only a few key people benefit, usually at the VP level or higher. This is incredibly toxic because it incentivizes upper management to look at every decision through a pure profit lens. They'll compromise their values to hit the next level because their vacation home renos are on the line.

We initiate profit sharing at 7.5 percent, and distribute it to all employees across every department. If you've been a Rethinker for over a year, you get a piece of the pie. Having a lower threshold (plus bigger pools unlocked at 10, 12.5, 15 percent, and beyond) means that most years everyone gets a cheque.

To determine who gets what, we give each department head a pool to divide up among their team. Most often, the money is split up equally. Sometimes outstanding individuals get a bigger slice, but fairness is always the goal.

It's important to manage expectations around profit sharing. When some people hear the words "profit sharing" they get dollar signs in their eyes. We make it clear that we're not a tech startup where people get tens of thousands of dollars. That said, a typical cheque might represent an amount double the rate of inflation, in relation to salary—which is nothing to sneeze at. Over the years, this has amounted to many hundreds of thousands of dollars in shared profits.

It's been money very well spent.

48 No Us vs. Them

Whether you're twenty-five employees or 250, everyone is on the same team.

There are two key challenges that we've tackled in an effort to foster unity and keep our company "one Rethink": eliminating departmental divides, and minimizing inter-office competition.

The primary challenge faced by creative companies, particularly ad agencies, is departmental divides. Many multi-national-owned companies take a siloed approach, in which strategists, account people, and creatives work separately. It's ostensibly for efficiency's sake, but creates an unhealthy dynamic where the suits are seen as the "parents" and the creatives as the "kids." Creatives will automatically react negatively to briefs they didn't have a say in crafting, and the account team will then blame those creatives for not sticking to the brief. It's adversarial, toxic, and promotes an us-versus-them mindset.

The only effective way to combat inter-departmental toxicity is to knock down the walls of the silos. An open-office concept can help with this, but it's not enough. It should start from the top—instead of having one president who's an account guy, Rethink has twenty partners and managing partners from across all departments.

Those departments need to be in constant communication, every day: Creatives get to weigh in on strategy. Account people get to weigh in on creative. Producers get looped in before the presentation.

Is it a lot of work? Yes. Is it a lot of meetings and check-ins? Also yes. But is it worth it? Hell yes. Communication is the antidote to competition.

Once a company gets big enough and expands into multiple offices, another challenge will emerge: how do you facilitate inter-office collaboration without pitting your offices against one another? Again, this is a problem that plagues multinational companies, where offices are routinely asked to "pitch in" on things for other locations—often without being paid, or with a promise that the other office will one day return the favour.

Why would any office want to help out on a pitch if they won't see a dime for winning it? This is one reason why Rethink's founders chose a more holistic profit approach. Each office manages their own P&L and gets rewarded for that performance. But the lion's share of the focus (and rewards) is on a consolidated P&L across all offices.

The benefits of the single P&L model are numerous and worthwhile. It allows the entire company to be more nimble and flexible. If Toronto needs a Vancouver creative team for a week, they can have them. If a Vancouver client needs French adaptation, they can tap into resources from Montreal. It fosters cross-country camaraderie and cheerleading—a win for one office is a win for all offices.

Avoiding the us-versus-them mentality isn't easy, but means less paperwork, less accounting, and most importantly, less conflict. It allows everyone involved to focus on the best solution rather than worrying about who's paying for it, which ultimately translates into better and more efficient work for the client.

49 DIY HR

Treat people like humans, not resources.

Rethink had an HR manager once. We'd survived many years without one, but when we reached seventy-five people or so, we wondered if we needed what every other company our size seemed to have. So we hired an experienced HR pro.

It did not go well. He was a nice enough person, but boy did he love rules. Binders and binders of them. Which we didn't have, so he wanted to create as quickly as possible.

We did what we always do, and rethought it. Instead of having traditional HR, we choose to distribute our company's HR tasks across our entire senior leadership group, across all offices, representing 165 employees.

When you hear that a company has "no traditional HR department," it might set off a few alarm bells. Who do people go to with sensitive information? Who can they report work-related grievances to? Who's going to stand up for them? How does it work?

Basically, it's all about division of labour. First, you need a broad senior management team. We have nearly twenty partners across three offices. Each office is run by two, three, or four managing partners picked from these ranks. The MP group represents the creative, business, and strategic sides of our business (see Shared Leadership, p. 195).

These partners take on all of the traditional duties of an HR department: interviewing and hiring new employees, conducting performance reviews, recommending salary adjustments, dealing with day-to-day frustrations, approving vacation days, and everything in between.

Second, all members of the group are empowered to make decisions on the spot (within reason), but they're also encouraged to table items for discussion with the group at large. It might sound daunting and time-consuming, but if you use common sense and share the labour, it's achievable… and surprisingly efficient.

Sensitive issues (like addiction issues or harassment) are dealt with by individual MP groups, with one or two partners taking the lead—usually those with the closest personal connection to the affected person. Sometimes this involves getting outside counsel from lawyers or therapists (we make sure we have local contacts for every office).

A word of advice: when dealing with any kind of HR issues, it helps to overcompensate whenever possible. Strive to be fair, impartial, and generous. Give every employee an annual review with honest, anonymous feedback, and an opportunity to review themselves (see Rethink Reviews, p. 69). Check in with employees regularly over coffee, spending as much time as it takes to ensure that they feel heard. Don't be stingy with raises—better to pay a bit more now than to find yourself searching for a replacement later. And if you do need to part ways with someone, do so with compassion and a generous compensation package.

Overleaf: Every Rethinker gets a bio and photo on our website. We supply the pedestal base; they supply the creative poses.
→

This approach is unconventional. It might not work for every size and type of organization, but it's worked for us. In addition to saving us money on HR salaries, it's allowed us to always maintain control over our culture and be more in touch with our people. It's made our leaders feel personally responsible and accountable for the well-being of every employee. And it's taken the concentration of HR power (and politics) out of the hands of one person or department.

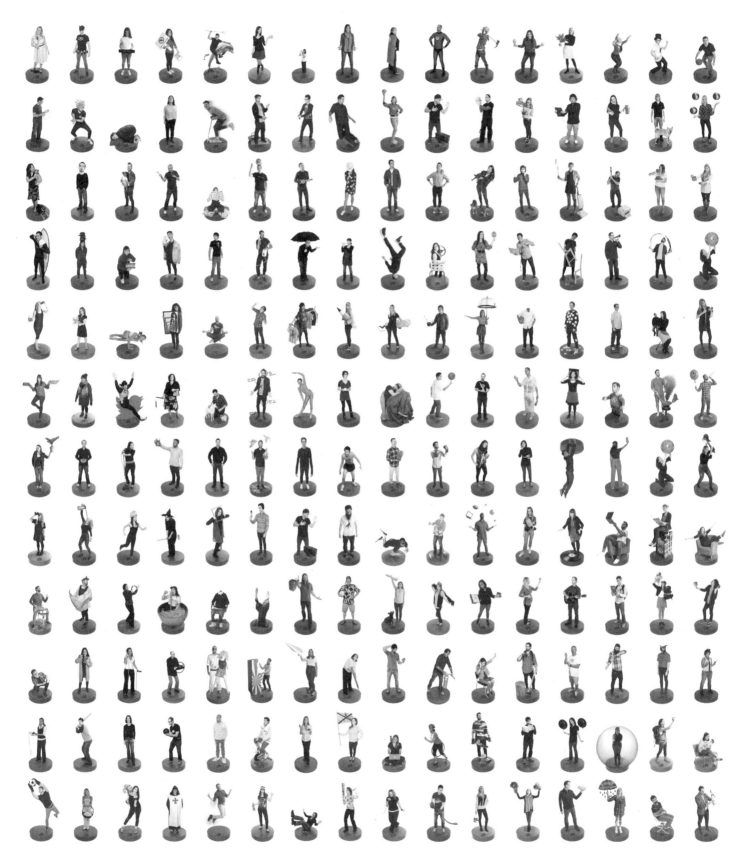

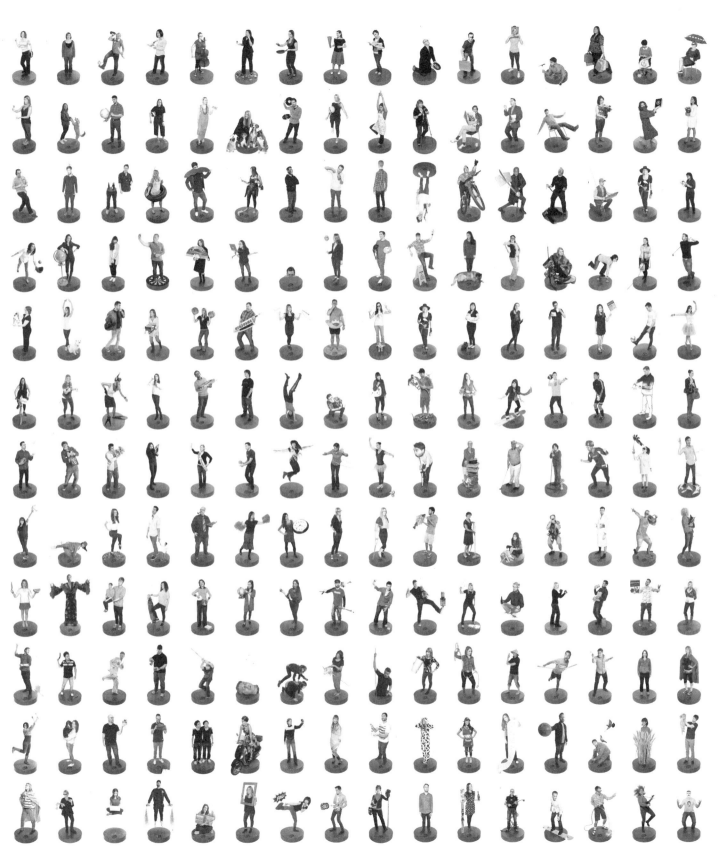

50 In-House Production

Want to save money and foster creativity at every level? Do it yourself.

In the past twenty years, the advertising industry has experienced massive disruption. It's shifted from a traditional media landscape with old-school production companies, to a digital-first world where everyone has an HD camera in their pocket. It's hard to justify a $300,000 video shoot to a client who believes they could shoot it on their phone. For agencies, this has meant a shift away from traditional advertising and toward top-to-bottom content creation in digital, design, and experiential channels—all backed up with fully integrated production capabilities.

Another source of disruption is the problem of attention. The thirty-second TV commercial used to be the gold standard of advertising, but captive mass-media audiences no longer exist. Now the goal is to stop someone's thumb as they scroll through their social feed. You have a fraction of a second to be interesting.

If you want to communicate a message to a large number of people, the sheer volume of content you need to produce has risen exponentially. You can't just shoot one video. It needs to be optimized for Facebook, YouTube, and Instagram. It needs to work as a :30, a :15, and even a :6. It most likely needs to work with or without sound. And of course you'll need vertical, horizontal, and square versions.

It didn't take us long to realize that relying solely on traditional production companies just wasn't going to cut it anymore. If we wanted to stay competitive, we needed to start our own production company. R+D Productions started out small, with one lonely video editor working on relatively minor projects in a corner of the office. But it grew more quickly than we'd anticipated, and within a year we found ourselves knocking down a wall to build more editing suites. We hired editors, motion graphics animators, visual effects artists, and colourists. We even trained a few of our writers to direct, which gives us total control over our final product and saves our clients from inflated director fees (not to mention the egos of A-list directors!). Seemingly overnight, we managed to turn one of our biggest expenses into a new profit centre.

Some people suggested that bringing production in-house too soon would weaken our product, but we've found the opposite to be true. Now our creative teams are able to be more involved in every stage of the process. If they want to work with an editor to solve a problem, they can just pop downstairs instead of taking a cab across town. This gives our staff a greater sense of responsibility and ownership over their projects—a very different mindset from the old model, where we would "hand off" an idea to a production company and let them run with it.

There are lessons here for lots of creative industries. Don't be afraid to try bringing things in-house. Start small and experiment (see R+D Days, p. 215). With today's amazing technological tools, you'll amaze your clients—and yourselves.

51 R+D Days

Tackle a fun creative problem by turning your entire office into a creative incubator for a day.

All creative businesses employ a wide range of people doing a wide range of things.

Some of these are classified as "creative," e.g., writers and designers. Others are seen as support services—like accounting or admin or production. We think that's an artificial divide that leads to wasted opportunities, and twice a year we prove it during company-wide R+D Days (or Rethink and Develop Days), when we put Rethinkers to work on a big, hairy creative problem.

Our inspiration came from "hack days" in the tech world—afternoons when developers drop what they're doing to work on new problems. Google famously allots a set number of hours a week for this kind of team thinking.

At Rethink, an R+D Day is a team-building event where we put our client work on pause across all three offices, form teams of four or five randomly chosen people, and spend a whole day tackling a creative problem. Subject areas are chosen to be topical, and can result in proofs-of-concept, working prototypes, even polished videos, depending on the brief. When social media became king a few years ago, we tasked teams with coming up with a single social post—a headline and visual only—that would cause an online sensation. Other R+D Day challenges have included:

- Identifying a pain point in our city and proposing a newsworthy solution;
- Combining any two concepts to create a third (see 1+1=3, p. 111);
- Building a working digital prototype that answers a human need;
- Producing twenty-five different styles of video around a common theme, like "lunch!";
- Proposing new ways to get young people to be more physically active; and
- Brainstorming ideas for this book.

After a day of exploring various concepts (and plenty of trial and error), teams share their solutions with the entire company via a short presentation. It's a pressure cooker, but the outcome is always surprising and inspirational. You'd be surprised at how many interesting talents, quirks, or secret passions lurk within your company's walls. Maybe your IT guy is a DJ. Maybe your CFO knows how to write code. Your temporary receptionist could be the funniest person in the office. You'll never know until you give them an opportunity. A great idea can come from anywhere, and everyone deserves their chance to be in the spotlight. R+D Day is the perfect time to tap into those talents and give everyone the chance to share their unique set of skills. Plus it's refreshing to hear some different voices in presentations for a change.

From a people perspective, R+D Day has an incredible galvanizing effect. You're giving people an awesome gift: the freedom to fail. Because it's not a paid client project, staff are more free to take risks and go with their gut. And because you only have a day, there's no time to conduct research or get hung up on the details. Forget about contingency plans, lengthy rollout discussions, messaging matrixes, or overbearing processes—you need this thing done, and you need it today.

By bringing together people from different departments to work on the same team (see No Us vs. Them, p. 205), on a new project with a tight timeline, you force them out of their comfort zones—a broadcast producer might find herself scribbling headlines; an account manager might get to be an illustrator for a day. This promotes divergent thinking, which lends itself to fresher ideas.[18] And it leaves zero room for ego. Collaboration and openness are the only way forward. (Be sure to take notice of which R+D teams thrive and which ones hit a wall; over time, you might begin to spot common denominators—see No Assholes, p. 21.)

In addition to being a fun way to get shit done, R+D Days will drive up the overall quality of your creative product. They break up the typical weekly routine, which can act as a hard reset for creative thinking. Plus, some of the ideas your teams generate on the day will actually be useable. Many pieces of work we've produced for our paying clients (including some of the work we're most famous for) started out as R+D Day proposals.

From a profit perspective, it's fair to point out that R+D Days aren't cheap. To an outside observer it probably sounds crazy to throw hundreds of non-billable hours at theoretical projects—not to mention the time and energy we spend planning each day, or the cost of feeding twenty-five teams (pizza ain't free!).

In our experience, however, the investment of time pays dividends. It breaks down departmental walls, which fosters teamwork and improves efficiency. It teaches teams to solve problems quickly and inexpensively by doing as much of the production as they can themselves. All of these things can be applied to our paying clients. R+D Days encourage a constant rethinking of how to solve problems, which reinvigorates our work and leads to long-lasting client relationships.

We believe that when you account for the shared learning and other intangible benefits, R+D Days are a profit centre. Though they might sound like a frivolous reality-show challenge, R+D Days are an invaluable tool.

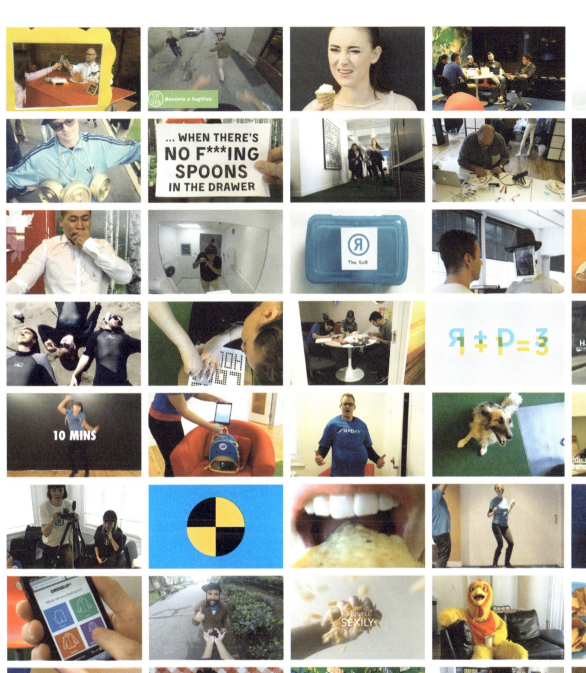

52 Change Proposals

Giving your people a creative outlet to solve important problems is good for them, and the bottom line.

Usually, a client comes to us with a problem and we come up with a creative solution. But Change Proposals, or CPs for short, turn the usual process on its head. With CPs, anyone can bring us any idea that they're passionate about, usually related to a not-for-profit enterprise, and that we can pull off on the cheap. If we believe in the power of the idea to turn heads or affect positive change, we'll go out and find the right client for it.

Every year, we invest two or three percentage points of our overall profit toward these projects. Think of it as profit put toward purpose. We've found that helping make positive change on a wide variety of purpose-driven projects really resonates with Rethinkers, especially the up-and-coming generations.

It isn't always easy. CPs require us to invest a ton of hours and cover the hard costs of the projects. We also have to reach out to companies (often cold-calling or emailing them out of the blue) to explain who we are, offer them the great idea—for free—and then reassure them that, no, this is not a scam. But the end result is an abundance of award-winning work for big-name clients who might otherwise never have heard of us.

Out of all the tools in this book, CPs might be the most unorthodox. Some people might see them as nothing more than an awards play, but many of the ideas we're most proud of and are best known for started out as CP scribbles on Post-it notes. Awards are one piece of the puzzle, yes. But they're merely a by-product of great creative problem-solving.

The moment a CP is approved it sends a spark through the entire office. Most CPs involve making something that's never been made before. A team of people from all departments comes together to do the impossible—and it's all for a good cause. Working in uncharted territory on a shoestring budget fosters unbelievable teamwork, often from unsung quarters. The hero in many cases is the account person who convinced a prospective client to back a CP, or the production manager who found a crazy inventor to create a breakthrough piece of technology.

For creative people, Change Proposals are perhaps our greatest motivational tool. Having an exciting creative project in the works keeps people energized and inspired, even if they're spending most of their time working on a Barge (see Barges, Speedboats & Submarines, p. 41). Creating buzzworthy work is a numbers game—nobody gets it on their first try. But CPs allow teams to swing for the fences over and over until they finally crank out a home run. Once a creative team "gets it," the home runs come more easily, the overall batting average rises, and the wins begin to pile up. And wins on CPs are the ultimate confidence boost. When someone experiences the thrill of seeing their idea break the internet and clean up at awards shows, they'll be driven to do it again and again.

The DIY nature of Change Proposals helps us foster a culture of innovation that improves the overall quality of our creative output. With CPs we get to try crazy, cutting-edge work with less fear of failure, and then apply our learnings to big-budget projects for our retainer clients. Because the not-for-profit clients tend to have little-to-no money for media and the production budgets are tiny, we have to be nimble and find ways to get more bang for our buck. Our paying clients certainly appreciate the ability to stretch a dollar—a strength that comes directly out of the testing ground that is CPs.

Although we've included them here in the Profit section, the truth is that CPs have a profound effect on every aspect of our business. Change Proposals are a secret weapon that perpetuates a cycle of success and leads to sustainable profitability. The buzz we generate with our little CP ideas helps us recruit and retain the most ambitious, most talented creative people out there. Those people help us raise the bar for our paying clients, which keeps them happy, which keeps us in the black. Many of our clients first heard of us through a CP idea they saw. And sometimes a CP idea will give us the foot in the door we need to build a longstanding paid client relationship.

If you ask any Rethinker about their favourite all-time projects, chances are it was a Change Proposal. When you give people the support they need to do breakthrough work for causes they're passionate about, you're enabling them to do the best work of their careers—at your company.

CPs

① PREDATOR WATCH MASKS

This series of posters for the Vancouver Police Department featured cops in kids' masks, referencing the department's efforts to bust online predators.

② ORKIN NOWHERE TO HIDE

Print advertising works best when it's dead simple, incredibly visual, and expertly crafted—like this ad warning bugs that with Orkin, they've got nowhere to hide.

③ SIX-SECOND AMBUSH ADVISORIES

Misogynistic music videos on YouTube rarely come with a warning. Until we created these six-second pre-roll ads for the YWCA matched to offensive videos aimed at kids.

④ GREENPEACE STOP SUCKING

These Instagram stickers allowed diners to tag a shot of a plastic straw with an overlay of a sea creature, in an effort to shame restaurants into switching to paper alternatives.

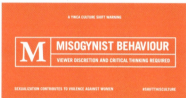

CPs

① **SIX-PACK ATTACK**

In 2010, we created this giant six-pack ring and placed it (without permits) on statues throughout Vancouver, starting a conversation on the perils of plastic in oceans.

② **DISTRACTED DRIVING POSTER**

There's nothing like a stripped down demonstration to make a point, in this case about the inherent difficulties (and dangers) of doing two things at once.

③ **THE PRIDE SHIELD**

To raise awareness for the International Day Against Homophobia and Transphobia, we worked with Fondation Émergence to create this installation of 193 LGBT+ flags (one for every country on earth). We then shot a .45 calibre bullet through the flags. A single flag stood no chance against the bullet. But the bullet lost power with each flag and eventually fell to the floor, showing that we still have to stand together to put an end to homophobia and transphobia.

53 Cherish Independence

Independence isn't just a business model. It's an attitude that pervades your whole company.

As Canada's only truly national independent agency, we at Rethink talk about the value of independence a lot. In fact, we often cite our independence as a key differentiator when we're pitching for new business. Nearly all of our competitors are owned by giant multinational holding companies, and are therefore at the mercy of the global head office's aggressive profit targets. Sure, they have massive reach and resources, but we believe that independence is an incredible strength—not just for us, but for any creative company.

Being independent allows companies to stay true to their core values, the ideals and philosophies that got them where they are. Only by staying independent can a company truly walk the walk when it comes to putting people first. At a multinational, profit always wins out. We place incredibly high value on the quality of our end product—which would surely suffer under the weight of relentless quarterly profit demands.

Speaking of profit, another massive advantage to being independent is having control over your margin expectations, and where you choose to invest profit. Want to invest back into your people through profit sharing or fun cultural events? Go ahead. Want to invest in passion projects, pro bono work for a not-for-profit, or turning an average piece of work into an award winner? You're the boss. Want to experiment and try new things? Schedule an R+D Day (p. 215).

One benefit of independence that many people underestimate is what we call "the power of no." As an independent, you can say no to a project that doesn't interest you. You can choose to part ways with a client who pays well but is kind of an asshole. Because you've invested in the best people and the best product, you can negotiate from a position of strength. And you'd be surprised how often a polite "no, thank you" can actually gain you respect, save you a world of headaches, and keep the door open for when the right opportunity does come along. Never underestimate the power of "no."

Finally, it should be noted that independence attracts and creates believers. The best and brightest independent thinkers (from creatives to planners to account managers) are often drawn to work for companies that share their values and ambition. And the best clients, the ones willing to take risks in the name of great creative, want access to those independent thinkers. Over time, the independent spirit of your company will become baked into your DNA, and your staff will be proud to be Davids in a world of Goliaths.

54 The Long Game

Adopt a long-term profit view—
year-to-year, not quarter-to-quarter.

Most publicly traded companies suffer from perpetual short-sightedness. They can't afford to step back and look at the big picture, because they're so fixated on their next quarterly profit report. And if a quarter doesn't look good, they react by prematurely selling assets, or cutting personnel and killing morale—anything to get the numbers up.

What does that do to a business driven by ideas? How can great ideas win the day in a penny-pinching environment? Friction and conflict between the two sides is inevitable. That's why we believe that running a business in three-month increments is insane.

We've been self-funded since the very beginning (we left some of our savings in the business as retained earnings), which has allowed us to avoid quarterly or annual reports to our financial institution. We do report to our partner group each quarter, but we always frame those conversations through a longer lens, evaluating the quarter against the fiscal to ensure we set ourselves up for a good year.

Another key differentiator is that instead of a fixed bottom line, ours is variable—we're always prepared to break even in a year when we can't achieve a higher level of profit. This is key, because it allows us to keep our team strong even after a lean year (even in our leanest year, however, we've always made money).

Because we're independent and committed to the long game, we're free to look at broader trends and make larger—some would say riskier—investments. When we expanded to Toronto in 2010, we were coming off one of our poorest quarters of all time. Imagine trying to break into a new market and open a new office while beholden to a quarterly quota.

The same could be said of our investment in production (see In-House Production, p. 213). The expense of building editing suites and hiring amplification specialists certainly put us at a short-term deficit, but it bought us security in the long term, and established two new profit centres in the process.

This long-term perspective also applies to our clients. We have several long-standing partnerships, clients that we landed in our very first year and have played the long game with—a strategy that is increasingly important to any company's sustainability.[19] We prefer ongoing partnerships over project-to-project gigs so that we can focus on growing our clients' business over time, not hanging everything on the success of a single campaign. That said, we never take any of our business for granted; each of our retainer contracts includes a notice period that could end the partnership in ninety days or less.

When you take off the blinders of quarterly thinking, you create a more sustainable company—one that can deliver profits for years to come, not just for three months.

Former Chiat/Day headquarters, designed by Frank Gehry, in Venice, Los Angeles. Despite the binoculars, few could foresee that the fiercely independent agency would be acquired by global holding company Omnicom in 1995.
PHOTO BY CHUCK PHILLIPS.
→

55 Rethinking Succession

Set your successors up for success with a plan that avoids selling out.

We're going to end this book on a personal note from Chris, Tom, and Ian, Rethink's founding trio.

Over the past twenty years, it's been incredibly challenging and rewarding to help build a strong and thriving creative company. As tough as it can be to build a business from the ground up, it can be even tougher to separate yourself from it when the time comes. Fewer than 10 percent of companies successfully manage succession.[20] Our biggest challenge has been figuring out how to let go, while ensuring that Rethink continues as a vibrant, independent company.

As founders and owner-operators, we've been deeply involved since day one. We spent the early years engaged in every aspect of the business, growing it and moving it forward. We learned by doing, took calculated risks, and managed to achieve consistent success (top ten among Canadian agencies for twenty years running). But that was the easy part.

At some point, we realized we couldn't stay involved forever. Being in our fifties with clients in their twenties just wasn't a particularly flattering or effective look. We found ourselves standing at a crossroads: we could sell Rethink to a multinational, abandoning everything we'd claimed to stand for as an independent… or we could make succession work on our own terms. Long story short, it was time to find a way to get out of the way (see Coaching 101, p. 79).

The first sign that our plan might actually work was when all three founders took ten-week sabbaticals in our tenth years, and others stepped up to ensure things ran smoothly without us. (Upon our return, we instituted tenth-year sabbaticals for all Rethinkers.) It seemed the more space we gave people, the more they would rise to the occasion. We realized that Rethink could survive perfectly well without our day-to-day involvement. That was when we committed to staying independent to the end.

After engaging the services of a corporate succession specialist, we worked out a phased approach to stepping back. Step one was identifying and grooming the next generation of leaders. A group of managing partners was selected in each office, with representatives from the creative, business, and strategic sides of the company. We invested in coaching the next generation, spending as much time with them as possible.

Next, we took a step back—from a highly involved day-to-day role into more of a coach/mentor role (this was a challenging step for a group that likes to get their hands dirty). We established Founder Facetime (p. 73) to ensure that everyone still had a chance to connect with us, plus bi-monthly updates with the MPs in each office, and quarterly sessions with our entire partner group.

After announcing and outlining the plan internally at an annual all-staff meeting, there was no turning back. The next move was a physical one: relocating from our high-traffic workspaces in the Vancouver office to a quieter space downstairs. The move sent a signal to the entire staff that the torch was officially being passed.

As time goes on we'll continue to reduce our presence in the office. We'll be available for select meetings, pitches, or events, but will operate in more of a board capacity. Over the years we've learned that being a good leader means letting others make the calls, and occasionally the mistakes. People learn by doing, not watching.

We recognize that our succession will work only if we put our full trust in the next generation, offering them guidance as needed, and then giving them the time and space to make it happen. We're also prepared to give them real skin in the game, in the form of gifted equity.

We can't wait to see what Rethink rethinks next.

Ian, Tom, and Chris

Shout-Outs

This book has been over twenty years in the making.

It represents the sum of everything we've "rethought" so far. As such, it is the result of dozens of people's contributions.

Many of the tools in this book first existed primarily as a verbal tradition, passed on from CD to creative team, and from Account Director to intern.

As our twentieth anniversary approached, we decided to codify the best of our thinking. We held an R+D Day to kick off the project, dividing the whole company into teams of four or five, across all departments. Each team was tasked with writing a chapter for this book, complete with some "fast and loose" ideas for accompanying visuals.

Much of that thinking remains in the final product. So we'd like to give a sincere shout-out to every Rethinker who contributed during that busy, exciting week.

To create a cohesive whole, we charged Rethink partner Morgan Tierney with the unenviable job of writing a first draft.

Thirty thousand words later, we arrived at a starting point for further visual exploration. We enlisted teams of creative directors, writers, designers, illustrators, and art directors right across the country to each take a chapter and refine and evolve the visual concept.

Thanks to everyone involved: Andrew Alblas, Eric Arnold, Alex Bakker, Marie-Sarah Bouchard, Charmaine Cheng, Julie Day-Lebel, Florence Dery, Karine Doucet, Dustin Gamble, Jake Hope, Evan Kane, Jordon Lawson, Jake Lim, Max Littledale, Liana Mascagni, Abrienne Miller, Sean O'Connor, Sheldon Rennie, Leia Rogers, Pamela Rounis, Maxime Sauté, Rob Tarry, Hans Thiessen, and Ashley Visvanathan.

Thanks to our research assistant Marie Horgan for tenaciously sourcing all of our notes and to Paul Budra for making Marie's internship happen.

Creating the final alchemy of words and visuals happened over the course of many weeks in Rethink's Vancouver studio. Thanks to everyone who touched the book here: Narine Artinian, Jonathan Cesar, Jan Day, Steve Holme, Linda Dumont, Ken Malley, Thomas McKeen, and Scott Russell.

Also, a special shout-out to our project managers, who kept multiple trains on the track at all times: Maddy Delage, Makena Heathfield, Alex Lefebvre, Aglaé Pagé-Duchesne, and Megan Park.

The team at Figure 1 Publishing deserves a special thanks for their input from start to finish. Their expertise helped us broaden the audience of this book to businesses beyond advertising and design. Thanks to Chris Labonté, Michael Leyne, Naomi MacDougall, Michelle Meade, Richard Nadeau, Mark Redmayne, Lara Smith, and Jessica Sullivan.

A final thank-you to our personal partners—Jennifer, Roxanne, and Steve—and to all the husbands, wives, and significant others who support us all day after day. Your advice and much-needed perspective have made all the difference.

Notes

1. "The Benefits of Bringing Pets to Work," MAPP Blog, University of Southern California, Online Master of Science in Applied Psychology, accessed 24 May 2019, https://appliedpsychologydegree.usc.edu/blog/the-benefits-of-bringing-pets-to-work/; and Lisa Evans, "Your Best New (Furry) Employee," *Canadian Business*, 21 June 2013, www.canadianbusiness.com/leadership/your-best-new-furry-employee/. The MAPP Blog post outlines how pets—usually dogs—in the workplace allow for improved work-life balance, stress reduction, and productivity. Examples come from companies such as Inverse-Square and Etsy that encourage pets in their workplaces, as well as from studies and surveys that prove how the potential risks of pets in the workplace (e.g., concerns about safety or allergies) are far outweighed by the benefits.
   International Take Your Dog to Work Day is the occasion for Evans's discussion of the effects of office pets on employee stress. Liz Palika, author of *Dogs at Work*, says "employees are generally happier with a dog in the workplace." According to a survey by *Modern Dog* magazine, 65 percent of readers would even accept less money to work at a pet-friendly office.

2. Bill Duggan, "The Five Biggest Trends on the State of Ad Agencies Now from the Digiday Agency Summit," Marketing Maestros (blog), Association of National Advertisers, 30 October 2015, www.ana.net/blogs/show/id/37368; Elliot Schimel, "Employees Crave Career Development. So Why Are Agencies Ignoring It?" *Adweek*, 13 March 2018, www.adweek.com/agencies/employees-crave-career-development-so-why-are-agencies-ignoring-it/; Elliot Schimel, "The 2.5 Percent Rule: A New Approach to Reducing Agency Turnover," Forbes Community Voice, *Forbes*, 7 December 2017, www.forbes.com/sites/forbesagencycouncil/2017/12/07/the-2-5-rule-a-new-approach-to-reducing-agency-turnover/; and Mark Wisniewski, "Turnover Continues to Cost Ad Agencies,"

NetSuite Blog, 15 November 2017, www.netsuiteblogs.com/turnover-continues-to-cost-ad-agencies.

Attendees at the 2015 Digiday Agency Summit wrote down the challenges they were facing in their respective agencies and posted them on the "Digiday Challenge Board." Employee turnover, according to Duggan, "had the most mentions, by far." The average annual agency turnover rate is 30 percent, and with companies like Deloitte, IBM, Accenture, and Epsilon beginning to offer marketing and agency consulting alongside their regular services, the talent market is becoming even more competitive.

In *Adweek,* Schimel investigates the causes of agency employee turnover (calculated by *ANA Magazine* at 30 percent on average) through the lens of how agencies are responding to millennial demands. "Millennials are looking for stability and a company where they can thrive," Schimel claims, but instead of "prioritizing professional development," agencies often ramp up office perks (e.g., Margarita Mondays). There's a gap, in other words, between what agencies think their millennial employees want and what those employees actually crave—hence the high turnover.

Schimel's concerns in the *Forbes* article parallel those in the article above, but here he spells out how agencies can tackle their turnover problem. To address the lack of professional development, which is often neglected in favour of "developing a culture that relies solely on perks," Schimel proposes that every entry- and mid-level employee should receive fifty hours of professional development sessions per year. (In a forty-hour work week, that would mean 2.5 percent of an employee's time.)

3. "Understanding the Stress Response," Harvard Health Publishing, Harvard Medical School, 1 May 2018, www.health.harvard.edu/staying-healthy/understanding-the-stress-response.

This article explains how the brain responds to and processes stress using the "fight-or-flight response." When the amygdala—the area of the brain that contributes to emotional processing—receives information that the individual is in a dangerous situation, it sends a distress signal to the hypothalamus (the brain's "command centre"), and from there our sympathetic nervous system activates. The article offers tips for countering chronic stress, such as relaxation, physical activity, and social support.

4. Albert Bandura, Bill Underwood, and Michael E. Froman, "Disinhibition of Aggression through Diffusion of Responsibility and Dehumanization of Victims," *Journal of Research in Personality* 9, no. 4 (1975): 253–69; John M. Darley and Bibb Latane, "Bystander Intervention in Emergencies: Diffusion of Responsibility," *Journal of Personality and Social Psychology* 8, no. 4, pt. 1 (1968): 377–83; and Michael A. Wallach, Nathan Kogan, and Daryl J. Bem, "Diffusion of Responsibility and Level of Risk Taking in Groups," *Journal of Abnormal and Social Psychology* 68, no. 3 (1964): 263–74.

In the classic study from Bandura et al., subjects were given the opportunity to behave punitively toward various test groups in scenarios with varying levels of personal responsibility. As the subject's sense of responsibility became more diffuse—i.e., when they didn't feel as personally responsible for the effects of their actions—their aggression increased. Diffusion of responsibility lessens productivity—which is the motivation for No Group Briefs (p. 39)—but when it causes aggression it can also impair camaraderie and cooperation.

Darley and Latane analyze the stakes of the "diffusion of responsibility" phenomenon in emergency situations, using the example of an individual having a seizure in public. They find a positive correlation between the presence of other bystanders and an individual's failure to help the victim; this correlation held regardless of gender. In other words, the more people who are present, the less likely it is that any of them—men or women—will intervene.

In their widely cited study, Wallach et al. conclude that when real risks and rewards are at stake, group decision-making leading to a consensus results in increased risk-taking—and that the reason is a diffusion of responsibility, i.e., each member of the group feels less responsible for the outcome than if they were making the decision on their own, and so are comfortable with greater risk.

5. Aloysius Wei Lun Koh, Sze Chi Lee, and Stephen Wee Hun Lim, "The Learning Benefits of Teaching: A Retrieval Practice Hypothesis," *Applied Cognitive Psychology* 32, no. 3 (2018): 401–10.

This study sought to understand why individuals learn better by teaching. Participants were divided up into four groups: a control group that solved arithmetic problems; one that taught without relying on notes, i.e., had to practice retrieving (or remembering) information; one that taught with notes (and therefore did not practice retrieval); and one that did not teach at all, but practiced retrieving information. In a comprehension test one week later, the group that taught without notes and the group that practiced retrieving outperformed those in the other two groups, suggesting that the learning benefits of teaching may be due to retrieval practice.

6. Ailsa C.M. Jerejian, Carly Reid, and Clare S. Rees, "The Contribution of Email Volume, Email Management Strategies and Propensity To Worry in Predicting Email Stress among Academics," *Computers in Human Behavior* 29, no. 3 (2013): 991–96; and Laura Marulanda-Carter, "Email Stress and Its Management in Public Sector Organisations," PhD thesis, Loughborough University, 2013, https://dspace.lboro.ac.uk/2134/14196.

Jerejian et al. surveyed 114 Australian academics to explore the causes of email stress. Individual propensity to worry and email volume were found to significantly increase stress, and email management did not help. The results suggest that email stress affects work performance, so any attempts at reducing employee stress should include email correspondence.

Marulanda-Carter studied email use at an unnamed organization in an effort to better understand the stress it causes, and develop strategies to counteract that. She found that email use led to increased physiological symptoms of stress, e.g., blood pressure, heart rate, cortisol, and perceived stress, as well as adverse psychological effects such as "social detachment, blame, and cover-your-back culture." There's no evidence that email-free time helps, but training participants in other strategies, like email filing and sticking to email schedules, showed some benefits.

7. Neil Patel, "The Psychology of Checking Your Email," HubSpot Blog, 23 September 2015, https://blog.hubspot.com/marketing/psychology-of-checking-email.

Patel cites multiple studies and experiments that demonstrate how email is distracting and stressful, and contributes to procrastination and "feeling let down." Nevertheless, people check email constantly and are often addicted thanks to the power of "operant conditioning," the simple principle of doing an action (checking email) and getting a reward (emails!). Limiting email to certain times helps reduce stress, and email marketers should keep these findings in mind when building campaigns, by including stress-relieving offers, for example.

8. Shawn Achor, "The Benefits of Peer-to-Peer Praise at Work," *Harvard Business Review,* 19 February 2016; and Josh Bersin, "New Research Unlocks the Secret of Employee Recognition," *Forbes,* 13 June 2012.

Achor looks at how to implement social recognition programs like those offered by Globoforce, where employees can post praise for their peers on an internal, company-wide newsfeed for everyone to see. Achor argues that allowing all employees to openly congratulate their peers, regardless of their status in the company, fosters a more productive and motivating office environment.

Bersin looks at employee recognition practices (e.g., giving gold watches, pins, thank-you awards, plaques, etc.) and identifies a glaring issue: rewards are generally based solely on tenure—employees "get rewarded for sticking around"—even when tenure-based rewards "have virtually no impact on organizational performance." But that system is changing, Bersin argues, drawing on *Forbes*' research on companies that score in the top 20 percent for building a "recognition-rich culture." These cultures foster a 31 percent lower voluntary turnover rate. A significant part of that culture is peer-to-peer recognition—both in-person from fellow employees, and on digital platforms like Globoforce or Achievers—which employees generally respond to more enthusiastically than top-down recognition.

9. Nicholas Bloom, James Liang, John Roberts, and Zhichun Jenny Ying, "Does Working from Home Work? Evidence from a Chinese Experiment," *The Quarterly Journal of Economics* 130, no. 1 (2015): 165–218.

This is perhaps the most widely cited study demonstrating why working from home works. To test productivity, Stanford researchers randomly assigned call-centre employees from Ctrip, a 16,000-employee, Nasdaq-listed Chinese travel agency, to work either from home or in the office. After nine months, employees working from home saw a 13 percent performance increase. Of this, 9 percent came from working more minutes per shift (fewer breaks and sick days) and 4 percent came from taking more calls per minute. The study attributes these gains to the quieter and more convenient home environment. Due to the study's success—and the additional qualitative benefits it found, like increased job satisfaction and employee wellness—Ctrip decided to allow all employees the option to work from home.

10. Shawn Achor and Michelle Gielan, "The Data-Driven Case for Vacation," *Harvard Business Review*, 13 July 2016; and Alexandra Sifferlin, "Here's How to Take a Perfect Vacation," *Time*, 7 August 2017.

Data collected in partnership with the U.S. Travel Association demonstrates that in the past fifteen years, employees have lost nearly a week of vacation time—by choice. Achor and Gielan suggest that the rise of time-saving technologies has, ironically, increased the amount of time employees spend working. This is partly due to personal devices making it harder to detach, but it's also a symptom of "productivity culture," which sees time off, even paid time, as detrimental to "getting ahead." But in 94 percent of cases, as their data reveals, vacationers return to work with more energy and a better outlook—which is why companies should be encouraging employees to take vacations.

Sifferlin discusses why vacations are necessary, and how to plan them effectively. "If planned poorly," she notes, "a vacation can actually lead to more stress." In a 414-person survey from the *Harvard Business Review*, nearly a third of participants who reported having "bad vacations" also admitted that their planning was rushed. Still, 94 percent of participants returned to work with as much or higher levels of energy, so Sifferlin insists that not only should employees take vacations, but they should take time to plan them properly so that they can experience the benefits of detaching from the workplace.

11. Graham Page, "Engaging Consumers' Brains: The Latest Learning," Millward Brown, May 2007, www.millwardbrown.com/docs/default-source/insight-documents/points-of-view/MillwardBrown_POV_Engaging ConsumersBrains.pdf.

When we encounter new objects or concepts, explains Page, our brains assess them according to three criteria: knowledge (what is it), experience (how is it used), and emotion (value-based associations). To be consciously aware of something, each of these three aspects must be assembled in our "mental workspaces" into a "representation." Our brains can only work on one at a time, and only three or four can exist in the workplace at once, so they are prioritized according to relevance and importance. While our brain is working on this there are moments when it "blinks," creating "blind spots" during which no new information can be processed.

For advertisers, this means that messages must engage each of the three criteria, and engage consumers at a time and place that allows them to be seen as relevant. And messages should be brief and clear—overwhelming audiences with brand-related messaging is counterproductive, since our brains simply cannot store that much content.

12. Lara Lee and Daniel Sobol, "What Data Can't Tell You About Customers," *Harvard Business Review,* 27 August 2012; and Alexandra Samuel, "New Data Reveals What Social Media Analytics Can't Tell You About Your Customers (Infographic)," Vision Critical, 14 April 2019, www.visioncritical.com/blog/social-customers.

Lee and Sobol address the trend of using "vast amounts of user-generated data to guide innovation of new products and services," and argue it does not amount to "customer intelligence," despite the faith of its many practitioners in nearly every industry. Data "reveals what people do, but not why they do it"—it provides no insight on human behaviour. Clorox adopted a human-centred rather than data-centred approach in developing their Green Works line of environmentally friendly cleaning products. Through in-home interviews and ethnographic studies they arrived at insights that "dramatically expanded" their market—insights that data mining could never provide.

Vision Critical analyzed the combined social media data and customer intelligence of three companies and found that although 85 percent of social media updates came from "enthusiasts" (customers who post five times or more per week), this group represented only 29 percent of a company's social media audience. In other words, much of the data represents a relatively small group. To maximize customer engagement via social media, companies also need to target customers who don't fall into the "enthusiast" category, such as "lurkers" and "dabblers."

13. David Cohen, "New Study Highlights How Much People Dislike Digital Ads," *Adweek,* 22 March 2018, www.adweek.com/digital/new-study-highlights-how-much-people-dislike-digital-ads/; Lauren Nettles, "New Data on Why People Hate Ads: Too Many, Too Intrusive, Too Creepy," VIEO Design, 6 September 2018, www.vieodesign.com/blog/new-data-why-people-hate-ads; and Daniel Newman, "Research Shows Millennials Don't Respond to Ads," *Forbes,* 28 April 2015.

Cohen writes about a study released by Instart Logic, a digital experience management platform, and Propellor Insights, a market research outfit, which surveyed more than one thousand adults and found they were generally "annoyed" with online ads. Whether on social media sites, retail sites, or news sites, respondents disliked how the ads interrupted content or led to website or app failures. Cohen doesn't use the word "hate," but it's clear that respondents were overwhelmingly in favour of sites hosting fewer ads.

As Nettles confirms, several recent consumer surveys speak to a popular belief that "advertising is only getting more pervasive, obnoxious, and intrusive": 87 percent of consumers feel there are more ads today than there were two to three years ago, and 91 percent of consumers feel that ads are more intrusive, with 79 percent feeling that they are being tracked by targeted ads. Some of the most common complaints are pop-ups, remarketing, and auto-playing videos. Many complainants do not call for all-encompassing ad-blocks, though, preferring that only the more "obnoxious" ads be blocked.

Newman discusses research that shows that the purchasing decisions of millennials are influenced less by campaigns than by their friends on social media. This distaste for ads, particularly targeted ones, has "turned the traditional marketing strategy on its head," Newman argues. Brands should respond by "creating communities" around their product (e.g., via Facebook) so that millennials can learn to trust the brand like they trust their friends and networks.

14. Adam Harden, "How Much Redundancy is Too Much Redundancy?" NASA Safety and Mission Assurance Directorate, November 2017; and Sean Michael Kerner, "What NASA Can Teach Enterprises About Redundancy," *eWeek,* 31 December 2013.

Harden's presentation explains how NASA implements technical redundancies for both safety and non-safety functions to ensure its systems are reliable. Harden looks at sample problems around communication lines between remote terminals and vehicle computers to test how the addition of a redundant train affects the probability of failure. He concludes that redundancies can improve reliability up to 93 percent.

Kerner explains how NASA astronauts Rick Mastracchio and Mike Hopkins removed a faulty ammonia pump on the International Space Station (ISS) and installed a new one, which was already aboard as a spare part. In space, "spare parts aren't easily sourced," so the station was built with the ability to accommodate inevitable equipment failures. Kerner stresses that even on Earth, companies should view redundancy as logical rather than as a luxury.

15. James Doubek, "Attention, Students: Put Your Laptops Away," NPR Weekend Edition Sunday, 17 April 2016, www.npr.org/2016/04/17/474525392/attention-students-put-your-laptops-away; William R. Klemm, "Why Writing by Hand Could Make You Smarter," *Psychology Today*, 14 March 2013; and Mark Murphy, "Neuroscience Explains Why You Need to Write Down Your Goals If You Actually Want to Achieve Them," *Forbes*, 15 April 2018.
Doubek describes a 2016 *Psychological Science* study from Princeton and UCLA researchers that compares students' retention of notes taken by hand or with a computer. The study finds that the "more selective" nature of writing notes versus typing them lends itself to "extra processing" of the material, and therefore higher retention rates. Because students type faster than they write, those using computers attempt to transcribe everything, which is too much information to process effectively—whereas hand-writers are more selective about what to record, and are thus able to process it more thoroughly.

Klemm reviews research on the relationship between learning cursive writing and cognitive development, particularly as it relates to "functional specialization, or the capacity for optimal efficiency." Brain-imaging studies reveal that as one writes, as opposed to typing, multiple areas of the brain activate, which trains different regions to work together, and help the brain to develop categorization skills. One study from Indiana University, for example, proved that the brain's "reading circuit" of linked regions activates during writing, but not during typing.

People who vividly describe their goals in written form are up to 1.4 times more likely to accomplish them than those who don't. The reason, Murphy says, is that it improves the process of "encoding," which is when the hippocampus analyzes information and decides whether to discard it or store it in long-term memory. Writing down your goals also reinforces what neuropsychologists call the "generation effect," where you better remember material that you generated yourself—by first generating the goal, then generating more details to write down, it "sears the goal into your brain."

16. R.A.E. Viney, J. Clarke, and J. Cornelissen, "Making Meaning from Multimodality: Embodied Communication in a Business Pitch Setting," in *The SAGE Handbook of Qualitative Business and Management Research Methods: Methods and Challenges*, edited by C. Cassell, A.L. Cunliffe, and G. Grandy (London, UK: SAGE, 2017), 298–312.
This chapter explores the theory of "multimodality" (the idea that meaning can be conveyed through non-language forms of communication) in the context of pitching business and campaign ideas. When companies pitch to clients and/or colleagues, the language used is manipulated—consciously or otherwise—by body language or other, subtler means. The authors argue that "speech and text are not necessarily seen as the dominant mode of communication," but instead as particular modes among many others, all of which interact to generate meaning—and in this context, to convince someone to get on board with an idea.

17. Tara Macleod and Oliver Wyman, "New Research Identifies How Star Performers Grow from Within," *Market Leader* no. 37 (Summer 2007); "What We Know About Internal Marketing and

Employee Engagement," WARC Best Practice, WARC, January 2019, www.warc.com/content/paywall/article/bestprac/what_we_know_about_internal_marketing_and_employee_engagement/112070; and Pini Yakuel, "Why Promoting from Within Works," Forbes Community Voice, *Forbes,* 20 June 2018, www.forbes.com/sites/forbescommunicationscouncil/2018/06/20/why-promoting-from-within-works/.

Macleod and Wyman describe a study that included a survey of over two hundred companies across the U.S. and Europe, and looked at how to create a workplace culture of "organic growth." Among the best practices identified is "build leaders to grow from within," rather than hiring executives from outside the company. If you work to improve the leadership capability of employees from the beginning, their potential expands, along with the company's profit and drive to innovate.

Internal marketing, by WARC's definition, involves both marketing employees and "any marketing communication efforts designed to appeal to prospective employees within the workforce." They offer eleven tips and tricks on how employees themselves can become "influencers"—and therefore "can make for highly effective brand ambassadors"—addressing how companies should view employees, how to empower them and engage them, and how ultimately this all benefits the company's internal marketing strategy and brand building.

Drawing on his experience as CEO of software development company Optimove, Yakuel offers two pieces of advice about promoting from within: "think of it like a marriage with a salary," and "embrace the mistakes." The first speaks to the importance of learning as you go: like a young person getting married, a newly promoted employee may not know exactly what they're doing, but if they're committed to learning and working together they'll figure it out—especially if there's an emotional attachment. The second recognizes the value of trial-and-error. Rather than search externally for the perfect match for the role, don't be afraid to try people in new roles. Worst-case scenario is you undo the move—but as you develop a keener sense of people's capacities that will happen less and less.

18. John Gruzelier, "A Theory of Alpha/Theta Neurofeedback, Creative Performance Enhancement, Long Distance Functional Connectivity, and Psychological Integration," *Cognitive Processing* 10, no. S1 (2009): S101–9; Erin Lamberty, "Recharging Creativity: How to Plan an Inspiration Field Trip," The Design Gym, 29 April 2016, www.thedesigngym.com/recharging-creativity-plan-inspiration-field-trip/; Ruth Richards, *Everyday Creativity and the Healthy Mind: Dynamic New Paths for Self and Society* (London, UK: Palgrave, 2018).

Gruzelier looks at the outcomes of using EEG-neurofeedback to increase the ratio of the brain's theta waves to alpha waves. The technique was originally intended to induce hypnagogia, the state between wakefulness and sleep that is associated with intense creativity. Gruzelier finds a range of beneficial outcomes, including enhanced music and dance performance, as well as a link between theta and alpha waves and a state of "meditative bliss," when regions of our brain interact in a way that optimizes performance and communication circuits. The connection here, in other words, is between relaxation and creativity.

Employee field trips are known to build community, but according to Lamberty they are also "essential to the creative process and keeping brains and workshops fresh"—as long as the activity is not directly work related, and is guided by a sense of adventure. Some examples she offers are meals at a restaurant, a virtual reality experience, or surfing.

Richards uses what she calls the "four Ps of creativity" (product, person, process, and press) to propose that creativity is inherent to all, and should be viewed as an everyday process, a "way of life." By combining a scholarly approach with personal encouragement, her book aims to help individuals understand the conditions that enable creativity, and how to encourage them in their lives.

19. Martin Guerriera, "Why Partnerships Are Proving Pivotal for Long-Term Brand Building," WARC Exclusive, WARC, November 2018, www.warc.com/content/paywall/article/warc-exclusive/why_partnerships_are_proving_pivotal_for_longterm_brand_building/124241; and Matthew Schwartz, "Keeping within the Lines: How Brands in Regulated Industries Keep Their Marketing Fresh," *ANA Magazine*, September 2016. Drawing on the 2018 list of BrandZ Top 100 Most Valuable Global Brands, Guerriera observes that many leading brands are able to raise the bar on customer experience by establishing "strategic, long-term partnerships" that allow them to survive market disruption by fostering "innovation and meaningful difference." BrandZ's research reveals that brands with high scores in these two areas grew by 11 percent annually, whereas brands with low scores declined by 37 percent.

Using Mike's Hard Lemonade as a case study, Schwartz explores "how brands can produce interesting, surprising, and fresh marketing ideas despite the many restrictions on what can be shown." For Mike's, these restrictions include a ban on over-consumption, and that all actors have to appear at least twenty-five years old. Vigilance is therefore key, and Schwartz's takeaway is that "regulations don't have to be roadblocks"—brands like Mike's (or brands in other regulated spaces, like cannabis, insurance, or finance) can use legal restrictions as a platform for creative surprises, or "twists," in their advertising.

20. "Business Succession Planning: Cultivating Enduring Value, Vol. 1: The Need for Planning," Deloitte Development LLC, 2015, www.deloitte.com/us/dges/BusinessSuccessionPlanning. Succession statistics are grim: using family-owned businesses as their example, this text says only 30 percent survive into the second generation, 12 percent into the third, and approximately 3 percent into the fourth (though these figures don't account for every company structure). In general, "many privately held businesses display solid professionalism and enviable profits in their daily operations," but they often "fail to properly plan for and complete the transition to the next generation of leaders"—and their business suffers as a result.

About Rethink

Rethink was founded in November 1999, in Vancouver, British Columbia, by Ian Grais, Tom Shepansky, and Chris Staples.

Rethink was created as an independent antidote to multinational agencies. Since the beginning, we've embraced a fully integrated model for solving communications problems—from strategy to advertising to design and digital.

A Toronto office was opened in 2010, followed by Montreal in 2015. Over the years, Rethink has been the most consistently awarded agency in Canada.

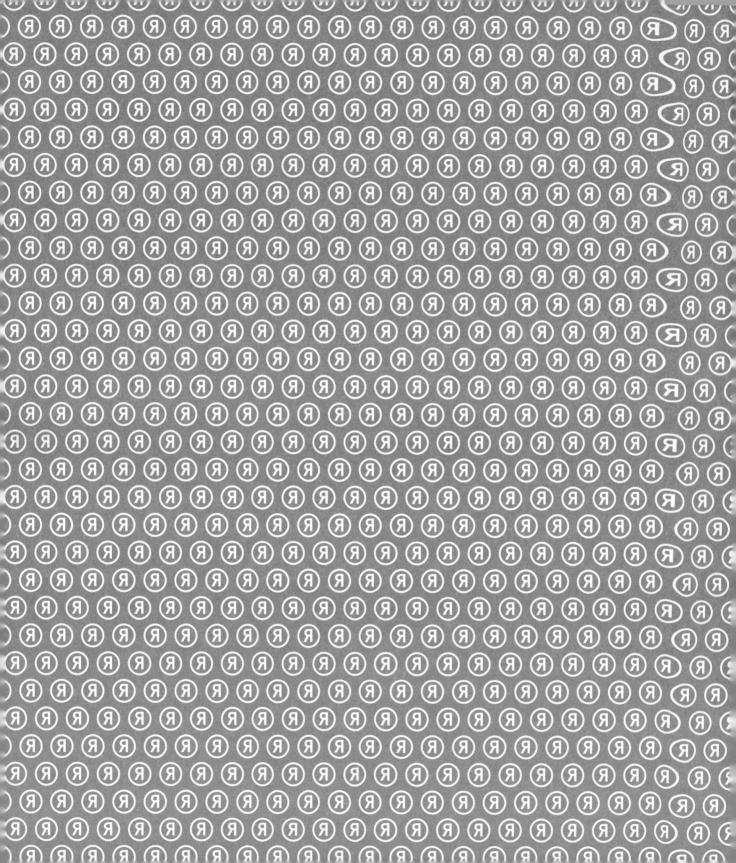